M000278015

10-Minute
Magic Spells

10-Minute Magic Spells

Conjure Love, Luck, and Money in an Instant

Skye Alexander

FAIR WINDS
PRESS
GLOUCESTER, MASSACHUSETTS

First published in the U.S.A. by
Fair Winds Press
33 Commercial Street
Gloucester, Massachusetts 01930-5089

Library of Congress Cataloging-in-Publication Data available

ISBN 1-931412-31-6

10 9 8 7 6 5 4 3 2 1
Cover design by Laura Shaw Design
Design by Anne Gram
Printed and bound in Canada

Note: The spells in this book are based on ancient tradition and are for
educational purposes only. The author and publisher assume no responsibility for any injury or damage caused or sustained while using the recipes
and rituals described in this book.

In memory of two women
who left this world too soon:

Jocelyn Edelston

MARCH 19, 1951 – AUGUST 15, 2002

Kathy McCoy

JANUARY 30, 1953 – JULY 29, 2002

✛ Contents ✛

Introduction

Part One

Part Two

Introduction

Magic is a mystery to most people. Some of them think it's all trickery, like stage illusion. Some consider it the stuff of myth, legend, or superstition, an anachronism in the twenty-first century. Others believe magic is evil, and that its practitioners are malicious sorcerers with strange, supernatural powers. Even individuals who may accept the reality of magic often view it as a rare and elusive art that's beyond their own capabilities.

All of these suppositions are false.

In truth, magic is real and it works. It is natural, widespread, and as relevant today as it was in King Arthur's time. Magic is not inherently dangerous or malevolent, but it can be misused by unscrupulous people, just as fire can be harmful in the hands of an arsonist. Although some individuals possess more native ability than others, virtually anyone can learn to perform magic effectively.

Magic, which often is spelled with a *k* to distinguish it from sleight of hand and other magic tricks, has been used by cultures around the world since ancient times. Some experts speculate that the animal images painted on rock walls by our cave-dwelling ancestors may have been a form of magic to petition the assistance of spirit animals during the hunt. Early agrarian societies often performed magical rites to ensure a bountiful harvest. Dancing around the maypole on Beltane (May 1), for instance, is an age-old fertility ritual performed at the beginning of the planting season.

The world's great religions are steeped in magical concepts and practices. The beliefs and practices of esoteric Judaism are based on the magical system described by the Cabala and the Tree of Life for transcending the physical realm and connecting with the Divine. That system also underlies Western ceremonial magic and the influential, century-old Hermetic tradition of the Golden Dawn, which laid the foundation for modern ceremonial magical work. Some Christian ceremonies, including baptism and Communion, are actually magical rites. Lighting a novena candle is a type of magic spell. So are chanting and prayer.

Many of our familiar customs and routines have magical ties. Undoubtedly, you've done magic yourself—you just didn't realize it. When you blow out candles on your birthday cake as you make a wish or hang mistletoe above a doorway, for example, you are performing simple magical acts originally meant to make your wish come true and banish evil, respectively. Magic is omnipresent, occurring all the time, everywhere.

How to Use This Book

In J. K. Rowling's Harry Potter books, young magicians go away to a special boarding school where they spend years learning their craft. Traditionally, aspiring magicians study the art of magic for extended periods of time and often apprentice with adepts before they are ready to practice on their own. Most of us don't have the time or opportunity to do this today, however. *10-Minute Magic Spells* is for modern, busy people who want to learn the fundamentals of magic so they can use it safely and effectively in their daily lives.

Part One covers the basics of magic, how it works, and how to use it successfully. This section also explains some of the special tools wizards, witches, and other magicians employ to enhance their work.

Part Two contains a collection of easy magic spells and rituals that usually can be done in ten minutes or less. I recommend that you don't jump ahead to this section until you've read Part One, unless you already know something about magic. In one sense, practicing magic is a little like driving a car—you need to understand the basic operating principles so you don't unintentionally harm yourself or others.

There's nothing difficult, peculiar, or spooky about magic. It is "extraordinary" only because modern human beings have lost touch with certain practices and teachings that once were part of ordinary existence. The magic in this book can be performed successfully even by beginners if they have the desire and dedication to do so. With practice, you'll become more proficient and your magic will become more powerful.

Part one, Chapter 1

Magic

Demystified

"Magick is not something you do, magick is something you are," writes Donald Michael Kraig in his book *Modern Magick*. Being a magician is more than doing a few spells or participating in a ritual, just as being a Christian is more than going to church on Sunday. Magic isn't something you put on and take off when the mood strikes you. It is a world view, a way of thinking and feeling and being—a way that contradicts much of what we in the West have been taught to believe.

To be a magician is to live in constant awareness of your connection with everything else in the Universe, knowing that you are in control of your own destiny. It involves all your senses, both the ordinary and the "extraordinary." A magician's world is a place of power and humility.

Magic is probably infinite in scope—there is always more to learn, so you will never know it all. And, just as it requires years of concentrated effort to become a marathon runner, master carpenter, or concert pianist, it takes time to become an accomplished magician. Don't let that intimidate you, however. You can begin doing elementary magic spells and rituals right away. As author Marian Green so aptly puts it in her book, *Elements of Ritual Magic,* "real magic is not a spectator sport."

For centuries, magical wisdom and occult knowledge were kept hidden, due to fear of persecution. (*Occult,* by the way, simply means hidden.) Magicians passed down secret teachings by word of mouth, through rituals, art, and coded texts. Numerology, which links each letter of the alphabet with a number, is one method used to convey occult truths to initiates while concealing them from the masses. The tarot is another. We have only now begun to rediscover the magic of our ancestors.

At the same time, contemporary magicians are putting their own spin on this ancient wisdom and adapting it to our twenty-first-century world. One example of this is the pairing of so-called complementary therapies in medicine. When herbal medicine, which draws upon the vital energies of plants for healing, is combined with modern medical technology and skills, this age-old magical art can produce results that surpass those known to early wise men and women.

Most of the magicians I know do magical work every day. Some magic is quite basic and practical, such as manifesting a convenient parking space at a mall on the Friday after Thanksgiving. Some of it is performed as part of an ongoing program of self-development, like daily meditation or exercise, rather than to produce a specific outcome. Other magical work seeks to achieve a goal, such as promoting healing, improving finances, or attracting a romantic partner. Once you become accustomed to using this "force," you will just naturally call upon your magical abilities to assist you in nearly every aspect of life.

An artist sees everything in terms of light and shadow, color and composition; a magician perceives everything in terms of energy. When you do magic, you tap the energies within yourself, in the earth, and in the worlds beyond. As you work with magic, you will begin to see things differently. Your relationships with other people may change, as may your relationship with yourself. You will experience the patterns and dynamics that underlie the superficial as you come to know that the physical world is only one part of the All. You will become aware of how your thoughts, words, emotions, and actions affect conditions in your life and you'll begin living more consciously. In short, magic will transform your life.

How Magic Works

When you work magic, you tap into the natural forces that exist all around us, on earth and in the heavens, and use them for a specific purpose. By manipulating energy, a magician creates the circumstances she or he desires. According to Aleister Crowley, one of the best-known magicians of the modern era, "every intentional act is a magickal act." More specifically, explains Donald Michael Kraig in *Modern Magick,* "magick is the science and art of causing change…to occur in conformity with will, using means not currently understood by traditional Western science."

Magic operates on the premise that everything is energy, and that everything in the Universe is connected to everything else. We exist in an energy matrix, which is like a giant web that entwines our Earth, our solar system, our galaxy, and beyond. When something happens in one part of the web, it sends ripples throughout the entire web—just as fluctuations in the New York Stock Exchange impact economics in Japan. This enables magicians to perform magic in their immediate environment and produce effects on the other side of the world.

The Universe contains numerous realms of existence, or levels of being, that interface with the visible world where we carry out our daily lives. We see only the tip of the iceberg, so to speak. By using intuition, imagination, and other mental powers that ordinarily lie dormant, we can access these unseen realms for magical purposes. We can communicate with the nonphysical beings who inhabit these levels of reality—fairies, angels, elementals, ancestors, and others—and gain their assistance in our magical work.

Types of Magic

Magic comes in many flavors. Some practices are complex, others are quite simple; there's something for everyone. Druid Magic, for instance, is closely linked with the natural world and the unseen parallel realms that interact with our own. Ritual Magic utilizes the Cabala and other teachings derived from ancient Mediterranean and Middle Eastern cultures to gain access to the higher realms; as the name suggests, this tradition emphasizes ritual and ceremony. Sex Magic channels erotic energy to produce specific effects. Shamanism involves interacting with nonphysical entities, such as ancestors, spirit animals, elemental forces, and deities, and moving between the various levels of reality. Wicca harnesses female and male powers, cosmic and earthly energies, to create what is desired.

These are only a few types of magic, and there are many others, each with its own unique focus, perceptions, rites, and origins. Some are culturally based. No one form of magic is "better" than another, although you will undoubtedly find some to be more appropriate for you than others. The magic I do is primarily based in Wiccan and neo-Druid traditions, because of my Celtic heritage, but I also blend feng shui, Eastern yoga techniques, and various other schools of thought into my practice. Although magic involves certain laws, it does not subscribe to any particular dogma—you can be a Christian, a Jew, a Buddhist, a Muslim, or without religious affiliation at all and still tread a magical path. An open mind is all you need to proceed.

Although I don't pretend to know about all the different types of magic, those with which I am familiar generally accept a few, fundamental concepts. Some of these are:

- There are many levels of reality and many planes of existence in addition to the apparent, physical one in which we conduct our mundane affairs.

- You constantly create circumstances with your thoughts, feelings, and actions.

- Your mind and intent are what empower your magical work, though special tools and rituals can enhance it.

- Magic is based in natural laws and works through the proper utilization of these laws.

Beyond these basic tenets, various magical traditions share lots of other ideas, even though their outer trappings may be different. For instance, many hold that a part of the Self (soul, spirit, higher self) lives on after the death of the physical body and may reincarnate again and again. Most believe in a Higher

Power and a Cosmic Order. For the most part, magicians honor all of creation and strive to live in harmony with the other beings on this planet, as well as with those that abide in the numerous unseen realms of existence. For more information about magical paths and traditions, read Bill Whitcomb's encyclopedic book, *The Magician's Companion.*

The Ethics of Magic

Many people fear magic and hold lots of misconceptions about it and its practitioners. That's not surprising, given the enormous "misinformation" campaign waged by religious, scientific, and political forces against magic for the past couple of millennia. Those practicing witchcraft, sorcery, divination, and other forms of magic have been punished with torture and death in many parts of the world. Even today, magicians tend to keep their beliefs and activities secret to avoid reprisal.

For the record, magicians *don't* worship Satan, put hexes on people, enslave unwilling individuals, or try to foist their beliefs on others. Magic is not dangerous if performed correctly. Magicians don't look different from other people. They aren't immune to life's problems. They have families and jobs and friends and, at least outwardly, seem pretty much the same as everyone else—the person who cuts your hair or repairs your car may be a magician.

Experienced magicians don't perform so-called "black" magic because they understand the ramifications of such acts. An important occult truth is that *whatever you do comes back to you*. Like a boomerang, the energy you put out in thought, word, or deed—good as well as bad—will return to you in kind. We see this law in operation in our everyday lives as well as in our magical lives. If you drive recklessly on the highway, for example, you may inspire road rage in other drivers. If, on the other hand, you smile at the people you interact with and treat them courteously, chances are they'll respond in a friendly manner. Of course, the repercussions of your actions aren't always this straightforward or immediate, but the law of cause and effect is immutable, and those of us who practice magic know that we cause the effects we experience.

This is not to say that magicians never misuse knowledge or behave irresponsibly. Many of us have. Magical power is a heady thing and, at least in the beginning, it's tempting to wield it selfishly. Some magicians say that novices can't really do much harm because they haven't developed the "magical muscles" to accomplish their objectives, and that once you reach a position of true power, you know enough not to abuse it.

To an extent, I agree. But I've seen inexperienced magicians get themselves into trouble by casting spells irresponsibly and calling up entities they couldn't handle. This can be very painful and disruptive to everyone—especially the spellworker. Love spells are where many people first get off track. They attempt to draw a particular person's love to them and end up binding themselves to the object of their affection. You should never manipulate another person. Instead, put out a "call" to the Universe that you are open to receiving a relationship that's right for you, and let Divine Will send you an appropriate partner.

The guiding principle behind Wicca is *do no harm*. If you follow only this rule, you will be moving in the right direction. When you realize that everything in the Universe is connected, you know that to hurt someone else is to hurt yourself. In a sense, that's what the Golden Rule is about.

To be on the safe side, it's a good idea to begin or end your magic spells with a statement such as, "Let this be done for the highest good, harming none." That way, you get your own ego out of the way and invite Divine Will to manifest your magic in the proper manner.

Magic isn't a toy. It is real and powerful and it works. Use it wisely, with love and respect. And remember the old saying, "Be careful what you ask for."

Chapter 2

Mind Over

Matter

Magic is "all in your mind." And it requires the use of all of your mind—all the different hemispheres, lobes, and nerves, the conscious and the unconscious, perhaps even those areas the purpose of which science hasn't discovered yet. When you do magic, you bring all your mental powers—your intuition, your imagination, and your concentration—to bear on a specific objective. The more adept you are at using these abilities, the stronger your magic will be.

Intent is the most important part of doing magic. Tools, words, movements, and clothing may help you to focus your mind, but they aren't the source of the magical force—you are. You can burn a green candle to attract prosperity, for instance, but unless this act is accompanied by your intention and fueled by your energy and enthusiasm, it won't succeed. "Magic cannot be successfully practiced without passion," Nancy B. Watson notes in her book, *Practical Solitary Magic.* The scene in *Harry Potter and the Sorcerer's Stone* in which the wand chooses the magician makes delightful reading, but it's not true. A magic wand is empowered by the magician's will—the only "life" it possesses otherwise is what's inherent in the natural materials (wood, metal, gemstones) from which it is made. (See Chapter 4 for more about magical tools.)

Magic is the art of consciously creating circumstances. "With our thoughts, we make the world," the Buddha taught. Dion Fortune, one of the instrumental figures in modern-day magic, said much the same thing when she wrote in *Sane Occultism,* "Events shape and take form on the Inner Plane long before they appear as actual happenings on the plane of manifestation in matter."

Before something can assume form in the physical world, it must first exist in the mind. Every physical creation, every building, book, film, painting, automobile, and software program started out as a vision in the mind of its creator. This is the essence of magic. When you perform magic, you first create a mental picture of an objective, and then you imbue it with energy. Your thoughts are the tools you use to shape your life. You are the architect of your destiny, designing reality according to your own plan.

The etheric plane is the subtle energy realm in which everything exists before it congeals into a physical form. Magicians project ideas, emotions, images, and energetic patterns into this parallel realm in order to generate effects in the physical world. I explain this further in my book, *10-Minute Crystal Ball*. The writings of Rudolf Steiner as well as other mystics and occultists provide detailed information about this and other realms of existence.

Magic, if done properly, always works. But this doesn't instantly happen with the tap of a wand or the twitch of a nose—that's another misconception arising from fairy tales and Hollywood depictions of magic. The physical world moves more slowly than the etheric plane does, so some details may have to be worked out or conditions put into place before the outcome you desire occurs. In some cases, it might be a few days, weeks, or even longer after you perform a magic spell or ritual before you see results.

Nor does magic generally happen in extraordinary ways. Leprechauns don't suddenly appear and hand over pots of gold. Prince Charming probably won't ride up on a white horse and carry you away to his enchanted castle. For the most part, magic operates through normal channels, without a lot of fanfare. Here's a story to illustrate what I mean.

In the spring of 2000, I wanted to get a mortgage to buy my house, but I didn't show enough income to qualify for a bank loan. I decided to do a magic spell in which I affirmed that I had enough money to purchase my home. (I'll explain more about affirmations shortly.) A few days later, I was visiting a friend when a real estate agent she knew stopped by unexpectedly. When I explained my situation, the realtor put me in touch with a real estate broker who enabled me to get a loan. I didn't win the lottery or find buried treasure in my backyard, yet my magic produced exactly the outcome I'd asked for.

Mental Clarity

Unless you know what you really want, you probably won't get it. In magic, a vague or muddled idea produces vague or muddled results. If you are "of two minds" about something, your divergent attitudes will neutralize and sabotage your efforts. Here's a good example.

A few years ago, I did a love spell for a woman who'd been single for a long time and wanted to meet a romantic partner. Months went by, but no new man entered her life. I'd done the spell correctly, so what was the problem? As it turned out, the woman planned to move to Italy. Her desire to move away and her desire to find a partner were in conflict. Some months later, she sold her house and relocated to Italy, where she promptly reaped the benefits of my spell!

Before you begin a spell, take the time to determine exactly what it is you want to accomplish. Be specific, but leave Divine Will enough leeway to produce results that are right for you. You may not know what's "right" or you might not be aware of all the possibilities that exist (or will soon exist).

Let's say, for instance, that you want a job as a teacher. Rather than doing magic to get a particular job at a particular school, you might perform a spell to find a job that allows you to share your knowledge with others, to work in a congenial environment with people you like and respect, to have convenient hours, and to be adequately compensated for your work. This way, the "great, cosmic job-placement agency" can scout around for something you'll really enjoy and maneuver you into that position.

Consider, too, the possible ramifications of your magic—how will the result you desire change your life? Are you prepared to accept these changes? Will other people be affected? If so, do you have their permission to interject your will into their lives? It is wrong to perform magic that interferes with other people's lives without their knowledge or permission, even if you have the best intentions. This is considered "black magic." Just to be safe, it's wise to end all spells with a statement such as, "This is done in harmony with Divine Will and for the good of all."

Finally, have faith in your ability to do magic. Doubt undermines success in any endeavor, and that's certainly true of magical work. When you perform a spell, don't question your methods. Don't redo the spell, "just to make sure." Don't worry about how matters will transpire. Trust that it will work in the proper way and at the proper time; then let it go.

Training the Mind

Most of us have trouble focusing our minds on anything for very long. We are an attention deficit disorder society. We're accustomed to "multitasking" and allowing our thoughts to jump from one thing to another like bees flitting from flower to flower. Try this experiment: Set a timer for one minute, then notice how many different thoughts you have during that brief period.

To do magic effectively, however, it's important to keep your attention on your objective. If you let your mind wander, you diminish the power of your magic and may inadvertently incorporate into your spell things you hadn't intended to.

Many of the steps that make up a magic ritual are designed to sharpen your focus, thereby increasing the amount of mental and emotional energy you bring to bear on your objective. Magic rituals serve a purpose similar to that of the centering rituals many athletes enact to improve their concentration and performance. Baseball player Nomar Garciaparra, for example, performs his lengthy ritual each time he comes up to bat!

Music, chanting, drumming, special movements, burning incense, and so on, influence your mental state and help you "get in the mood" for magic. Some people find that dressing in ritual clothing or donning special jewelry prepares them mentally, enabling them to temporarily leave their ordinary world for a magical one. Meditation, deep breathing exercises, or yoga can be beneficial preliminaries to doing magic. The point is to rein in a restless mind, empty it of distractions, and direct it toward a specific intention, and whatever technique works for you is OK.

Visualization is used in a lot of magical work. This mental exercise involves forming a clear picture in your mind of the outcome you wish to achieve through your spell. Choose a vivid picture that has strong emotional appeal for you and awakens your enthusiasm.

In protection spells, for instance, magicians often visualize themselves (or someone else) surrounded by a ball of white light. In spells designed to promote healing, the injured area is visualized as being healthy and whole. When I want to stir up my creativity, I imagine a wise woman stirring a huge cauldron filled with enticing ideas over a crackling fire. Use your imagination to create a vision that's meaningful to you and embellish it with color, action, texture, scent, sound—whatever things make it richer and more real for you. Just as a sculptor sees the statue within a block of marble, you should visualize the end result, not the condition as it currently exists or the steps between here and there.

Affirmations are another key ingredient in many magic spells. An affirmation is a short, positive statement that describes the condition you wish to achieve. If your goal is to attract prosperity, for instance, you could create an affirmation such as: "My life is now rich with abundance of all kinds." Be sure to use the present tense when wording your affirmation; otherwise you may delay results indefinitely.

Gestures also play a part in many magic rituals and spells. These movements often symbolize the intention or outcome you wish to bring about. An open hand might represent being receptive; an arm held up over your head could signify drawing down energy from the heavens.

Spells are frequently performed within a protective circle, which prevents outside interference and keeps the power of your magic close at hand until you are ready to release it. Magicians traditionally cast a circle by "drawing" it in the air around the perimeter of the area in which the magic work will take place. You may use a ritual dagger (known as an *athame*), a magic wand, or your finger to draw the circle. This symbolic movement reinforces your visualization and helps to prepare you mentally for the task at hand.

Symbols in Magic

"Symbols aren't just handy shortcuts, like the icons for gas stations and restaurants that we see on highway signs," I wrote in *Magickal Astrology.* "They are images that express the essential nature or quality of something because they also embody its essence." Our world is awash in symbols, and whether or not we realize it, they impress themselves and their inherent meanings on us at a deep level.

Advertisers intentionally incorporate symbols into their imagery to trigger positive, subliminal responses to their products. In the days before most people could read or write, religions conveyed messages to their followers through symbols—we see these in church and temple decorations as well as in the rituals enacted during religious services and ceremonies. The Star of David is an ancient and powerful symbol; so is the Catholic gesture called making the sign of the cross.

Some symbols, such as circles, crosses, and spirals, are universal—we find them in the artifacts of cultures everywhere, dating back to preliterate times. Others are societal or personal, and may mean one thing to me and another to you. You can even create your own unique symbols.

Symbols encapsulate your purpose and speak directly to the subconscious, which is why they can be powerful adjuncts to magic work. Symbols also communicate information to other people. Numbers, letters, geometric shapes, astrological glyphs, and pictures (such as hieroglyphs) are some of the most common symbols used by magicians. Magical tools—wands, candles, chalices, pentagrams, and so on—are potent symbols, too.

Many of the spells in Part Two of this book call for the use of familiar symbols, and I'll explain them as we go. But rather than discussing them at length, I suggest that you refer to my book, *Magickal Astrology* or another good book on the subject for more extensive information about the meanings of symbols and their magical uses.

Circle Casting

As I mentioned earlier, magicians usually perform spells and rituals within a protective circle. Circle casting is the most fundamental and frequently used magic ritual. The circle keeps unwanted energies outside and holds the magic you generate inside until you are ready to release it into the world. Inside the magic circle, you are separated from the ordinary, mundane world within a space that is considered sacred—treat it appropriately.

Before you start, disperse any vibrations that might disturb or interfere with your magic work. Sage is often burned to "smudge," or cleanse, the area. Witches sometimes sweep the space with a broom, but you may clear it by simply brushing unwanted energies away with your arms or by visualizing the area filled with purifying white light.

There are many ways to cast a circle. The easiest is to envision a circle of white light like a wall surrounding you and the area in which you will be working. If you prefer, you can use your finger, an athame, or a wand to symbolically draw the circle. Start at the easternmost point of the area in which you'll be working. Then, holding your tool in your left hand with your arm outstretched, walk clockwise around the circle you wish to secure, so that when you have finished you are enclosed within the space.

To cast a circle using the four elements, light a stick of incense (which symbolizes fire and air) and hold it in your left hand as you walk clockwise around the circle from the east. Next, sprinkle saltwater (which represents water and earth) along the edge of the circle as you walk clockwise, again from the east. (I'll discuss the four elements in more detail in the next chapter.) Experienced magicians may use more complex and dramatic rituals, but these basic circle-casting techniques will work just fine.

Once the circle has been cast, you shouldn't leave it unless it's absolutely necessary, and no one else should enter the circle. If you must leave, use your finger or athame to symbolically cut a doorway in the circle. Step through the opening, then "close" it by drawing the doorway again, but in reverse. When you reenter the circle, repeat these movements. (It's generally believed that cats can enter and leave a circle whenever they choose without observing this formality!)

After you have finished your magic spell or ritual, open the circle. Begin at the east and walk counterclockwise, with your arm outstretched, until you return to your starting point. As you do this, imagine that you are removing the protective barrier you erected earlier. When you have finished, with your right arm pointed up at the sky and your left arm pointing down at the ground, say, "The circle is open, but unbroken."

Chapter 3

Heaven

and Earth

The positions of the Sun, Moon, planets, and other heavenly bodies influence conditions here on Earth, from the ebb and flow of the tides to the development of personality throughout life. They also affect the magic you do. In magic, as in other aspects of life, timing can make the difference between success and failure. By coordinating your magic with favorable solar, lunar, and planetary cycles to work with the prevailing forces rather than against them, you can enhance its power and effectiveness.

Making the Best of Celestial Cycles

Lunar phases, in particular, play an important role in magical work. The new moon is a time of beginnings; the full moon brings matters to fruition. Magic that instigates growth or increase, such as prosperity spells, should be performed during the moon's waxing period (between the new and full moons). As the moon becomes bigger and brighter, so will whatever you initiated during this phase. The waning moon (from full to new) supports magic that involves endings or decrease. This is the time to do spells to lose weight, break an old habit, or end an unsatisfactory relationship.

The equinoxes and the solstices are especially powerful times for working magic. You can also take advantage of the sun's position in the various zodiac signs to augment your magic. Each of the twelve signs is linked with certain matters, so, if possible, perform spells when the sun occupies the sign related to your intention. For instance, the period when the sun is in Taurus (from about April 20 to May 20) is a good time to do prosperity spells. Rex E. Bills' *The Rulership Book* provides extensive lists of the areas connected with each of the signs, but here are few to get you started.

Aries		men, sports, conflict, vitality, action, beginnings
Taurus		money, gardening, art, music, fertility, sensuality
Gemini		communication, short trips, mental pursuits, education
Cancer		home, family, children, women, real estate
Leo		self-expression, leadership, leisure, games of chance, love affairs
Virgo		health, work, coworkers, pets, routines

Libra	♎	partnerships (love and business), legal issues, art, social occasions, beauty
Scorpio	♏	hidden matters, investments, other people's money, transformation, sex, the occult
Sagittarius	♐	long distance travel, higher education, religion, publishing
Capricorn	♑	business, authority figures, structure, elders, boundaries
Aquarius	♒	friendship, groups, technology, change, anything unconventional
Pisces	♓	intuition, liquids, sleep, imagination, music, ocean voyages, endings

It's also a good idea to perform certain types of magic on certain days of the week, for each day has its own unique energy. That's because each day is governed by one of the celestial bodies. For instance, Monday, which is the moon's day, would be ideal for doing a spell to bless a new home. By combining the appropriate daily and monthly energies, you improve your prospects for success.

ON...	RULED BY...	DO MAGIC FOR...
Sunday	Sun	Creativity, leadership, fame
Monday	Moon	Home, family, intuition, fertility
Tuesday	Mars	Sports, vitality, action, sex, men
Wednesday	Mercury	Communication, intellect, travel
Thursday	Jupiter	Growth, luck, travel, prosperity
Friday	Venus	Love, joint ventures, women
Saturday	Saturn	Limits, reduction, permanence

For more about which types of magic are best done during each period and for information about planetary hours, see my book, *Magickal Astrology*.

Invoking Celestial Powers

Magicians sometimes utilize the energy of the Sun, Moon, and planets in magical practice by "invoking" one or more of the heavenly bodies and inviting them to empower a particular spell. This may be done by actually calling out your request to the heavenly body, by using ritual gestures, or by visualizing the body whose energy you wish to "borrow" while you work a spell. Or, include its astrological symbol in a magical mojo (a talisman or amulet). Some of the spells in Part Two use this technique.

Earth Magic

According to astrological theory, everything on Earth is ruled by one or more of the planets or "luminaries" (the Sun and Moon). The ancients believed that a particular god or goddess inhabited each of the planets and presided over specific matters on Earth. Venus was in charge of love and relationships. Neptune governed the oceans and all that transpired on the seas (shipping, fishing, and so on).

Earth reflects heaven, or, as the old axiom goes, "as above, so below." It all goes back to the concept I discussed in Chapter 1—everything in this magical Universe we live in is connected to everything else by a complex network of vibrations. Two things that are different in form may be related by virtue of having similar vibrational patterns. It's easy to see the link between pearls and oysters. But if we look a little further, we find that pearls are the birthstone for the zodiac sign Cancer and that Cancer is the sign astrologers associate with shellfish.

You can incorporate celestial energies into your magic spells by using the plants, gemstones, and objects from nature that are ruled by the appropriate planets. This type of "nature magic" is popular among followers of Wicca and other earth-honoring spiritual traditions. When you get to Part Two, you'll find a number of spells that make use of this system.

The list below shows some planet–gemstone–plant relationships. Many books offer more complete information than I can here, so if you decide to pursue magic seriously, you will want to add to your personal library some of the comprehensive titles listed in the Resources section on page 243 of this book.

HEAVENLY BODY	STONES	PLANTS
Sun	ruby, amber, tigereye	sunflower, dahlia, marigold, poppy, saffron, chamomile
Moon	moonstone, pearl	iris, water lily, willow, jasmine, hyssop, watercress
Mercury	aquamarine, agate	azalea, honeysuckle, lily of the valley, valerian, lavender, dill
Venus	opal, coral, turquoise, emerald, rose quartz	columbine, orchid, almond, bergamot, peppermint, rose, apple, raspberry, strawberry
Mars	bloodstone, diamond, carnelian	cumin, cayenne, mustard, onion, snapdragon, oak

HEAVENLY BODY	STONES	PLANTS
Jupiter	turquoise, topaz, sapphire	sage, magnolia, sandalwood, olive, chestnut, clover, mint
Saturn	onyx, smoky quartz, jet, obsidian	holly, carnation, mistletoe, hemp, pine, moss, hops
Uranus	garnet, zircon	carnation, ginseng, clove, cinnamon, nutmeg, wild rose
Neptune	amethyst, aquamarine	violet, wisteria, narcissus, lotus, water lily, iris
Pluto	bloodstone, lodestone	eucalyptus, foxglove, rye, chrysanthemum

Chapter 4

Tools of the Trade

Whether they're power saws or computers, most of us employ special tools in our jobs that enable us to work more effectively. The same is true for magicians.

The practice of magic utilizes four main tools: a wand, a dagger (known as an *athame*), a chalice, and a pentagram. Each tool represents one of the four elements (fire, air, water, and earth, respectively) and each has a distinct purpose. In addition, many magicians use candles, crystals, incense, bells, scrying mirrors, swords, cauldrons, oracles, essential oils, and various other tools. Strictly speaking, you don't need any of these— your mind and will are the forces that generate magic, and the rest are just accoutrements. But these tools can be valuable assets because they help you focus your mind and create an environment that's conducive to working magic.

The Four Principal Tools

Magical tools possess no inherent power—until you infuse them with your energy, spirit, and intention. This is done by "charging" them in ritual fashion, which I'll explain shortly. After you charge your tools, they become your faithful servants and should not be handled by anyone else without your permission. But first, let's look at the tools themselves and how they can augment your magical work.

✣ Wand ✣

Considered by some to be the most important tool in the magician's toolbox, the wand represents the element of fire and the spirit. "Wands" is also one of the four suits in the tarot (some decks call it "rods"). Tradition says that a wand must be at least six inches long. Although it is often made of wood, virtually any material is acceptable. I have a beautiful magic wand made of sea-green glass and adorned with numerous semiprecious gems. I also own a couple of handsome gemstone miniwands that are good for traveling and double as pendants to hang from a necklace. You can fabricate your own wand or purchase one ready-made.

The wand's long, pointed shape directs energy. Magicians use wands to draw down power from the heavens and to focus it wherever they choose. Often, a magician will cast a circle with his or her wand (see the section on circle casting in Chapter 2). But you wouldn't tap someone on the head and turn him or her into a toad—that's only done in the movies!

✤ Athame ✤

This ritual dagger represents the element of air and the intellect, and is depicted in the tarot as the suit of swords. Usually, the dagger features a straight, double-edged blade about four to six inches long, but some witches prefer a curved athame that resembles a crescent moon. The important thing is that yours feels comfortable in your hand.

Unless you possess skills as a metalsmith, you probably won't make your own athame. Be certain to get one that has never drawn blood; although old weapons may be attractive, it's probably safer to purchase a new dagger. Some years ago, I found an elegant knife in an antique store that I initially thought might make a terrific athame—until the shopkeeper told me it had previously served as a rabbi's Brith knife! I now use a handsome serpent-headed dagger from a company that replicates museum pieces.

An athame's principal purpose is to banish unwanted energies from an area. It can also be used to cast a circle. Generally speaking, you don't cut anything with it except symbolically, so it needn't be sharp. (Use regular kitchen knives to chop magical herbs and flowers.)

✛ Chalice ✛

Symbol of the water element and the emotions, the chalice appears as the suit of cups in the tarot. Your chalice can be made of any material you choose—silver, glass, porcelain, wood, et cetera. The chalice is used to hold liquids that a ritual's participants drink. Because the chalice may be handed from person to person, one with a long stem that's easy to grasp is preferable.

✛ Pentagram/Pentacle ✛

A five-pointed star that often is enclosed in a circle, the pentagram represents the element of earth, the body, and the material world. In the tarot, it appears as the suit of pentacles or coins. This tool is frequently worn in the form of jewelry, though some magicians like to display decorative altarpieces or wall plaques depicting the symbol. One of the pentagram's roles is to protect you while you perform magic.

Other Tools

Only you can decide which tools to include in your magical collection. Your choice will depend on the type of magic you do and your personal preference; it's a bit like determining which software programs best suit your purposes. Candles and incense are the magical staples, and many of the spells I provide in Part Two involve these popular tools. I frequently use essential oils, quartz crystals and gemstones, and oracles in my practice, too. But I don't own a sword (which is generally considered to be a man's tool) or a scrying mirror (I prefer my crystal ball for gazing into the future). To help you make up your mind about which tools are right for you, here are descriptions of some of the most common magical tools and their uses.

✛ Grimoire ✛

Also known as a "Book of Shadows," a grimoire is a magician's private spell book. Here you record your spells and rituals, along with pertinent information such as the date you did the spell, the moon's phase, time of day, and, of course, your results. Although I share some of my own spells in Part Two, usually you'll want to keep your grimoire's contents secret.

✛ Candles ✛

The word "candle" comes from the Latin *candere,* meaning *torch.* Candles play roles in many of our favorite religious and secular rituals, as well as magical ones. Blowing out candles on a birthday cake, for instance, is a popular tradition, but it's also a simple magic spell, intended to make a wish come true and bring good luck in the coming year.

Candle magic may be the most common and widespread form of magic; it's included in many, if not all, magical traditions. In the practice of magic, candles represent the element of fire and the spirit or life force. This tool can be used as a focusing aid, for scrying, to represent people or higher powers, and for many other purposes.

Often magicians inscribe candles with words or symbols that relate to their intentions. If you are doing a love spell, for example, you might carve a heart or the word *love* into the candle wax. As the candle burns, your intention is dispersed into the Universe and set into motion. You can even get creative and form candle wax into a symbolic shape to represent a person, object, or intention.

The candle's color can contribute to your spell, because each color exhibits certain properties and characteristics. Many candles today are also scented with essential oils, which combine magical qualities with sensory and psychological benefits. If you prefer, you can "dress" candles yourself by anointing them with the essential oils that are appropriate for your spell or ritual. When you incorporate color and scent into your spells, you involve several senses in your work and enhance the power of your magic.

The following lists of color and scent associations will help you select the candles you need:

Magical Color Correpondences

COLOR	INTENTION
red	passion, vitality, courage
orange	warmth, energy, activity, drive, confidence
yellow	creativity, optimism, enthusiasm
green	healing, growth, fertility, prosperity
light blue	purity, serenity, mental clarity, relief from pain
royal blue	loyalty, insight, inspiration, independence
indigo	intuition, focus, stability
purple	wisdom, spirituality, power
white	purity, wholeness, protection
black	power, the unconscious mind, banishment, boundaries
pink	friendship, affection, joy, self-esteem
brown	grounding, permanence

Essential Oils and Their Magical Connections

INTENTION	OILS TO USE
love	rose, ylang-ylang, patchouli, musk, jasmine, bergamot
prosperity	pine, cedar, peppermint, clove, cinnamon, sandalwood
protection	basil, fennel, sage, myrrh, amber, frankincense, verbena
intuition/insight	narcissus, lavender, wisteria
purification	camphor, sage, pine, rosemary
healing	lemon balm, balsam, sweet birch, frankincense, myrrh, ginger

✛ Essential Oils ✛

Anointing is a sacred ritual in many religious and cultural traditions. In Greek, *anointing* means *the Holy Spirit poured out,* and in Hebrew, the word for Messiah translates as *anointed one.* In ancient Egypt, the bodies of rulers were anointed to preserve them and fragrant oils were placed in their tombs for use in the next dimension.

Essential oils are pure plant extracts in highly concentrated form. Not all perfumes or scented candles contain these oils, however, and synthetic fragrances lack the energetic and magical properties inherent in pure, botanically derived essential oils. In addition to dressing candles with them, essential oils can be added to a ritual bath, used in magic potions and mojos, or worn to stimulate the senses. Some of the spells in Part Two tap the powers of essential oils.

✛ Incense ✛

The ancients called incense the *breath of God.* Incense burning began in Japan around 600 B.C.E. and remains an integral part of many rituals in the East. In Buddhist ceremonies, a statue of the Buddha is considered to be merely a piece of sculpture until incense is burned as an offering—then the inert figure is transformed into the Buddha himself.

Incense, in Latin, means to sacrifice or make sacred. Magically, burning incense represents the combined elements of fire and air. The fragrant smoke stimulates the limbic center of the brain, triggering psychic and emotional responses that contribute to the magician's intention. Incense is used to purify sacred space, cast a protective circle, and charge magical tools (see below). Magicians also burn it when they want to send messages to the deities: As the smoke rises toward the heavens, it carries your request with it.

You can purchase incense already scented for specific purposes. Or, you can perfume your own with essential oils. The list on page 53 shows which scents are appropriate for various types of spells.

✛ Crystals ✛

The word *crystal* generally refers to quartz, although many other stones also have crystalline structures. The ancient Greeks named these stones *krystallos,* meaning ice, because they believed the gods had frozen water eternally into these naturally faceted, sunlight-refracting gems. According to legend, the magicians of Atlantis harnessed the sun's energy with crystals to generate power for the entire continent. It's even speculated that crystals were used to focus energy so that the pyramids and Stonehenge could be built.

Crystal workers consider quartz crystals to be living entities possessing a unique form of intelligence that can be tapped for working magic. Prized for their ability to retain information, crystals can be "programmed" to carry out your intentions. They also amplify the energies of other stones and herbs, so adding a piece of crystal to a magical mojo increases its power. When affixed to the end of a wand, pointed crystals focus, heighten, and direct energy. Crystal balls are popular scrying devices, but all crystals can be used in this manner.

Quartz crystals come in many "flavors," and each has its own distinct strengths. Smoky quartz possesses exceptional memory and stabilizing properties. Rose quartz emits gentle, loving vibrations. Citrine (usually pale amber or yellow) promotes cleansing and purification. Only natural quartz crystal can be used in magical work—leaded crystal is not alive.

✛ Gemstones ✛

Although today we treasure gemstones for their beauty and monetary value, originally they were prized for their magical powers and worn to attract good luck, health, courage, protection, love, and so on. Birthstones offered numerous benefits because they harmonized with the wearer's astrological sign.

Because stones are very dense and hold onto energy for a long time, they are ideal for magical work. Each gemstone is imbued with its own special qualities, which you can harness by wearing them or including them in magic spells and mojos. The following list shows some popular gemstones and their magical uses.

INTENTION	STONES TO USE
love/friendship	rose quartz, coral, opal, diamond, emerald, pearl, peridot
prosperity	aventurine, jade, tigereye, turquoise
protection	amber, jade, malachite, tourmaline
healing	jade, jasper, agate, bloodstone, amber
intuition/insight	amethyst, lapis lazuli, moonstone, opal, aquamarine, sapphire
stability/grounding	onyx, hematite, jet, obsidian, smoky quartz
courage/vitality	carnelian, ruby, topaz, garnet, diamond

✤ Oracles ✤

For thousands of years, wise men and women have sought guidance from oracles such as the *I Ching,* tarot, runes, and astrology. Oracles are tools that help us to tap into our own inner guidance and to connect with other realms of consciousness. They bridge the gap between the known and the unknown. They enable us to gain insight into other people, to see what's going on beneath the surface of perplexing situations, and to get information about the future.

Because oracles contain powerful symbols that the subconscious intuitively understands, they can also be used as focusing aids or to represent your intentions in magic spells and rituals. The Lovers card from the tarot, for instance, could play a role in a love spell. In Part Two, I include some spells that incorporate glyphs from the runes and the *I Ching* into magic mojos.

My book, *10-Minute Crystal Ball* provides a brief overview of several oracle systems. If you aren't familiar with divination tools, I suggest consulting a good book on one or more of these oracles before attempting to use them in your magic.

✦ Cauldron ✦

Usually associated with witches and feminine power, this tool symbolizes the water element, creativity, and fertility. Cauldrons may be used to prepare magical brews and potions. Sometimes ritual fires are built in cauldrons.

✦ Bell or Gong ✦

Used to stimulate the sense of sound, bells and gongs often signal the different steps or stages in a ritual.

✦ Sword ✦

Like the dagger, the sword is usually used to banish unwanted energies or to symbolically cut through obstacles.

✛ Sigils ✛

Sigil comes from the Latin *sigillum,* meaning sign. A sigil is a symbol that contains letters, numbers, and/or images interwoven to create a picture. You design this magical symbol to express your intention in graphic form, for two good reasons. First, the subconscious responds better to pictures than to words. And second, because no one but you can understand your sigil's meaning, you can write your desire in secret code.

Start by PRINTING the individual letters of a word or short phrase that describes your intention, such as *P, R, O, S, P, E, R, I, T, Y.* Eliminate any duplicated letters—in our example, the second *P* and *R.* Now, configure the letters into a design that pleases you. The letters can be positioned upright, upside down, backwards, normally—in any way you choose. Use uppercase or lowercase letters, or a combination of both. If you wish, embellish your design with other symbols that reinforce your intention, for example, dollar signs, hearts, runes, or astrological glyphs.

You can display your sigil in a prominent place, to remind you of your intention. Or, you can incorporate it into a magical mojo or another type of spell. I sometimes include sigils in my paintings—and I even know people who have gotten sigil tattoos. In Part Two, I include some spells that use sigils.

✢ Scrying Devices ✢

Scrying is the art of seeing beyond what normally can be perceived with the physical eye. Crystal balls are popular scrying tools, but any shiny surface will work, including a black mirror, a pool of water, or the hood of a well-waxed automobile. The device itself does not actually contain any power, it merely allows your "inner sight" to open up and project images for you to interpret.

Charging and Caring for Magical Tools

When you "charge" a magical tool, you imbue it with energy generated by your own will. You also consecrate the tool for special magical purposes, in much the same way religious implements are "blessed." Different magical schools follow different procedures, some of which are quite elaborate. If you wish, you can even create your own ritual for charging your tools. Once again, the most important factor is your intent. Here's a simple, standard, and effective ritual you can do in less than ten minutes:

1. Wash your tools with water and dry them to cleanse them of any unwanted vibrations.

2. Collect incense and something to burn it in, saltwater (if you live near the sea), or water, and a little salt or soil.

3. Cast a circle within which to perform your ritual by following the instructions in Chapter 2.

4. Hold your tool in the smoke of the burning incense as you say aloud: "I now charge you with fire and air."

5. Sprinkle your tool with a little water and salt or soil as you say: "I now charge you with water and earth." (NOTE: Salt will tarnish metal, so if you are using tools made of silver, brass, et cetera, you may want to dust them with a little soil or ashes instead.)

6. Envision your own energy and power flowing into your magical tools as you perform this ritual.

7. Repeat this procedure with each tool.

8. Gently wipe your tools to remove excess water, soil, et cetera.

9. Open the circle. Your tools are now ready to do your bidding.

10. Wrap your tools in silk or cotton cloth and store them in a safe place when they are not in use.

Part two, Chapter 5

Love

Spells

Friday is usually the best day to perform love spells, so unless otherwise noted, the spells in this chapter should be done on a Friday. If your intent is to attract a new partner or strengthen an existing relationship, work the spell during the waxing moon. If you want to end an unfulfilling partnership or diminish something connected to a relationship (such as the pain of a broken heart), perform the spell during the waning moon.

Before you begin, take a few minutes to relax, center yourself, and clear your mind of any distractions. To ensure your protection, envision a ball of white light surrounding you and the space you're working in, or cast a circle according to the method outlined in Chapter 2.

Many of the spells in this chapter use candles or fire. As a commonsense precaution, don't leave candles or ritual fires burning when you aren't there to tend them. If you build a fire in the course of working a spell or ritual, do it in a safe place—a fireplace, woodstove, barbecue grill, or other site designed for this purpose. Some magicians kindle small fires in heavy iron cauldrons, but remember that a cauldron gets very hot, so handle it carefully. Many spells recommend letting candles burn down completely. If this isn't possible, however, extinguish them by snuffing rather than blowing them out.

Although it is often tempting, it is never right to manipulate another person or to work magic that will cause anyone unhappiness; such attempts usually backfire and may result in unpleasantness for the spellworker. If your spell involves someone else, ask his or her permission first. Perhaps you'd like to invite this person to join you in performing the spell. If you cannot secure the other individual's permission, don't include him or her in your spell—unless the spell is intended to make peace with another person or to break an unwanted bond between you. Instead of trying to make a particular person love you, use your magic to attract a partner who is right for you. That way, everyone wins.

✥ Burn a pink candle to attract love.

Pink is the color of love and affection. If you want to attract new love into your life, dress a pink candle with rose essential oil (see Chapter 4 for more information). Light the candle and let it burn down completely. Be sure to put it in a safe place, and don't leave home while the candle is burning.

✥ Burn a red candle to increase passion.

We associate the color red with passion, so this is a good spell to do when you want to turn up the heat in a relationship. Carve the word "passion" in a red candle. The day after the new moon, light the candle and let it burn for ten minutes, then snuff it out. Repeat this every day until the moon is full or until the candle has completely burned down.

✿ **Burn two candles to bring you and a partner together.**

Choose two red or pink candles and place them about a foot apart. One candle represents you, the other symbolizes your partner. Light the candles and let them burn for ten minutes, then snuff them out. The next day, move the candles a little closer together (the exact amount doesn't matter). Light them and let them burn for ten minutes, then snuff them out. Repeat this every day until the candles are touching, and then let them burn down completely.

✿ Burn incense to improve your love life.

Incense is often burned to send prayers to the deities. Light a stick of rose- or jasmine-scented incense. While it burns, ask Venus, Aphrodite, Freya, or another love goddess to help you improve your love life. As the smoke rises up to the heavens, it carries your wishes along with it.

✿ Sleep on it.

Fill a small, pink cloth pouch with dried red-rose petals. Dot the pouch with rose, ylang-ylang, jasmine, or patchouli essential oil. Put the pouch under your pillow at night to attract new love into your life.

✿ Write a love letter.

Imagine the type of person you want as a partner. Instead of thinking about a specific person, envision the qualities you desire in a lover: intelligence, a good sense of humor, compassion, reliability, and so on. Now, write a letter to this prospective partner, telling him or her how much you admire and enjoy these characteristics and how happy you are to have found someone who possesses them. Also describe what you can offer in the relationship. When you have finished, fold the letter three times and kiss it.

Build a fire in your cauldron (or a fireplace, woodstove, or barbecue grill), and include some apple wood or cedar as fuel. You may be able to purchase fragrant woods in stores that sell fireplace, grilling, or smoking supplies, or through mail order or online catalogs. Drop the letter in the fire and allow it to burn completely to release your request into the Universe.

✿ Let Rumi's poetry enhance your love.

The Persian Sufi poet, Rumi, wrote hundreds of beautiful and powerful love poems in the thirteenth century. To the Sufis, Divine love and human love are interwoven—human love enables us to know Divine love and Divine love is expressed through human relationships. Read the poetry of Rumi and copy down a poem that strikes a chord in you. Each day, read the poem aloud while you focus on expanding your capacity to give and receive love. This practice helps to open your heart and sends loving vibrations out into the cosmic web. If you wish, you may read the poem to a partner.

✿ Use a tarot card to attract love — Spell 1

Perform this spell on the first Friday night after the new moon. Choose the Lovers, the ace of cups, or the two of cups from a tarot deck. Lay the card face up on a windowsill where it will receive the moon's light. Wash a small piece of rose quartz and place it in your magical chalice or a glass. Fill the chalice with water and set it on top of the tarot card overnight to absorb the card's vibrations. In the morning, remove the rose quartz from the glass and drink the water.

✡ Use a tarot card to attract love — Spell 2.

Begin this spell on the first Friday after the new moon and repeat it each day until the full moon. Choose the Lovers card, the two of cups, or the ace of cups from a tarot deck. Position the card so that you can see it. Light rose-, jasmine-, patchouli-, or musk-scented incense. Stare at the tarot card for ten minutes while the incense burns and repeat an affirmation such as: "I am now united with a partner who is right for me and we are very happy together."

✵ Use a tarot card to attract love — Spell 3.

Choose the Lovers card, the two of cups, or the ace of cups from a tarot deck. (NOTE: This should come from a deck you don't ordinarily use, as you won't return the card to the deck when you've finished working the spell.) On a piece of pink paper, draw a love sigil according to the instructions in the following spell. If you'd like to, you can embellish your creation with symbols that represent love to you. Put the sigil behind the tarot card, then place both of them together in a picture frame so that the card faces out. Hang your spell in your bedroom or someplace where you will see it often. If you know feng shui, display it in your Relationship Gua.

✿ Create a love sigil.

Configure the letters *L, O, V,* and *E* into a design that you find appealing. The letters can be positioned upright, upside down, backwards, sideways, or in any other way you choose. Use uppercase or lowercase letters, or a combination of both. When you've finished creating your sigil, hang it in a place where you will see it often. Each time you look at it, you'll be reminded of your intention to increase the amount of love in your life. If you prefer, you can incorporate your sigil into a magical mojo. (For more about sigils, see Chapter 4.)

✿ Heal a broken heart.

Cut a heart out of a sheet of red paper. Tear it in two pieces, then stick the pieces back together again with an adhesive bandage. As you do this, say or think the words: "My heart is completely healed and I am happy again." Put the paper heart in a green envelope that's large enough to hold the heart without folding it and place the envelope in a bedroom drawer until your heart no longer aches.

✿ Make a spicy love charm.

You'll need:

- a stick or cone of rose-scented incense
- a circle of pink cloth (preferably silk), 6 inches in diameter
- a 6-inch length of red ribbon
- a pinch of marjoram
- a pinch of sage
- a pinch of cumin
- a pinch of paprika
- a pinch of celery seed
- a small amount of dried raspberry leaves, stems, or fruit

Light the incense. Place the last six ingredients in the center of the circle of cloth. Tie up the cloth with the ribbon, making six knots. Each time you tie a knot, say or think the words: "I now have a lover who is right for me in every way." When you have finished, hold the charm in the incense smoke for a few moments. Carry the charm in your pocket to attract your soul mate.

✿ Make a botanical love charm.

You'll need:

- a small jar or bottle made of clear, green, or pink glass
- 2 red or pink rose petals
- 2 myrtle or violet petals
- 2 pink clover petals
- 2 petals from a blackberry, strawberry, or raspberry flower
- 2 apple or cherry blossom petals
- 2 small, pink pearls

Place the petals and pearls in the bottle. As you do this, hold loving thoughts in your mind to help you attract a new lover or to increase the love between you and your current partner. Stopper the bottle with a cork, if possible, and seal it with red sealing wax. If this isn't possible, stopper the bottle with red cloth or tissue paper. Place the bottle in your bedroom window on the night before the full moon to attract love.

✿ Make a magical love mojo.

You'll need:

- a piece of parchment (or good-quality writing paper)
- a pen with red ink
- rose, jasmine, patchouli, or ylang-ylang essential oil
- a small box with a lid
- a piece of red or pink ribbon
- a silver ring or a round silver earring
- a small piece of rose quartz
- a shell
- an oval or elongated smooth stone

Write an affirmation, such as, "I now have a lover who is right for me in every way," on the parchment with the red pen. Put a drop of essential oil on it and fold it three times. Place the paper in the bottom of the box, then put the last four ingredients in the box. Close the box and tie it with the ribbon. Make six knots and repeat your affirmation each time you tie a knot.

If you wish, you can decorate the box with images, such as hearts, that suggest love to you. Store the mojo in a night-stand or dresser drawer.

✡ Make peace with a partner.

Perform this spell to restore harmony if you've had an argument with a partner. Envision you and your partner together in a happy, peaceful state while you draw a yin–yang symbol on a piece of paper. Write your name in one half of the symbol and your partner's name in the other half. Dot the paper with rose essential oil. Slip the symbol in an envelope, then seal it with pink sealing (or candle) wax. Impress a heart or another favorite symbol of love into the warm wax. Mail the letter-spell to your partner.

✿ Take a magical love bath.

This easy and enjoyable spell can be a prelude to an evening of romance or a nighttime ritual to attract new love. Make yourself a cup of hot raspberry or blackberry tea while you fill the bathtub with water. Add a few drops of rose, ylang-ylang, jasmine, or patchouli essential oil to the bath water. If you like, you can sprinkle rose petals in the water, too. Light a pink or red candle. Play soft, romantic music. The key is to involve all your senses in the process. Sip your tea and soak as long as you like. While you bathe, think loving thoughts.

✧ Make your own magical massage oil.

Start with a base of a cup or so of almond, grapeseed, or olive oil. Add a few drops of one or more of the following essential oils: rose, jasmine, ylang-ylang, patchouli, bergamot, vanilla, clove, musk, or nutmeg. When the scent pleases you, pour the oil into a clear or green glass bottle. Affix the label that you design in the following spell to the bottle of oil, making sure the pictures are facing in, against the glass (so they infuse the oil with their power). To increase the passion between you and your partner, massage each other with the special oil you've formulated.

✿ Create a magical love label.

In magic spells, symbols and pictures are often used to influence the subconscious. On a small piece of pink or red paper, draw symbols and pictures that represent love to you. If you wish, you can also write words, a phrase, or a poem about love. As you work, keep your mind focused on thoughts of love. The finished product can be used as a label for your own, custom-blended massage oil (see the previous spell). Or, simply display your creation in a place where you will see it often.

✿ Make your own rosewater.

Do this spell the night before the full moon. Fill a large bowl (preferably one made of copper, silver, or porcelain) with water. Scatter pink or red rose petals onto the water and set the bowl in the moonlight overnight. In the morning, strain out the rose petals and bottle the water. Use the rosewater to dress candles, sprinkle on love talismans, or to add to bathwater. (NOTE: The best roses to use are ones that have been given to you by your lover.)

✡ Bring a lover to your door.

Here's another way to attract a lover with your magical rosewater. Dip your finger in the rosewater and with it, draw the symbol for Venus on your forehead. Then, pour the rest of the rosewater on your doorstep, or if you live in an apartment, rub some on your doorknob and/or doorbell. In your mind's eye, see a lover walking up to your door and knocking. Make this vision as vivid as possible, but don't imagine a particular person in this role— allow the Universe to bring you the lover who is right for you.

✡ Make three loving wishes come true.

You'll need:

- a piece of pink ribbon 18 inches long
- scissors
- a red or silver pen
- jasmine, rose, ylang-ylang, patchouli, or musk essential oil

Cut the ribbon into three 6-inch lengths. Write one wish on each piece of ribbon, making sure to word them in a positive manner and in the present tense. When you've finished, braid the ribbons together while you think about your wishes or chant them aloud. Dot the braid at both ends and in the middle with essential oil. Place the ribbon charm on your altar, in a nightstand drawer, or under your pillow to make your wishes come true.

✿ Use an opal to make a wish come true.

According to gemstone lore, opals are very sensitive to your emotions and respond to your energies. Sometimes called "Cupid's stone," they are also associated with love and romance. Wash an opal in cool water (preferably a stream or other natural body of water, although running tap water will work if that's all you have at your disposal). Hold the stone in your left hand, close your eyes, and focus your attention on your heart's desire. Send loving feelings from your heart, down your left arm, and into your hand, where the opal will absorb them. When you feel a tingling sensation or warmth in your hand signaling you that the opal is ready to respond, make a wish. State your request in a positive manner and use the present tense. But remember the old saying: Be careful what you wish for!

�֍ Wear carnelians to stimulate passion.

The name *carnelian* comes from the Latin for flesh, hence the stone's connection with physical pleasure. These vermilion-colored stones increase vitality, self-confidence, and passion, so they can be worn to restore youthful virility or improve your sex life. Hang a large carnelian on a gold, silk, or leather cord so that it rests against your heart. Or wear a whole string of carnelian beads to kindle desire and enthusiasm.

✡ Create a gemstone talisman to boost your love quotient.

Several gemstones are prized for the loving vibrations they emit. Rose quartz encourages affectionate feelings and harmony. Carnelian stimulates passion. Jade enhances stability, loyalty, and joy in relationships. Coral promotes fertility. Pearls balance emotions and smooth out the rough spots in a relationship. Opals inspire romance and help make wishes come true. Malachite opens your heart and increases your capacity to love. Moonstone makes you more nurturing and accepting of others. Choose the gems that best suit your purposes, then string them together. Wear this talisman or carry it with you to bring out these qualities.

❈ Plant a romantic garden.

Flowers are closely connected with love and romance. In the Victorian era, each flower had a particular meaning and lovers sent floral "letter" bouquets to express their feelings. You can encourage romance by cultivating flowers that are associated with love—roses, violets, gardenias, jasmine, myrtle, red clover blossoms, primroses, and columbines. Choose red or pink flowering varieties, when possible. Place a small piece of rose quartz in the ground or flowerpot, then set the plant on top of it. Care for your flowers with devotion: Talk to them, play music for them, feed, water, weed, and prune them. The attention you lavish on them symbolizes the care you give to your relationship. As they grow strong and healthy, so will your love.

✿ Seek relationship help from the west.

West is the direction magicians associate with emotions and matters of the heart. You'll be petitioning the archangel Gabriel, guardian of the west, for assistance with this ritual. If possible, perform this spell while the moon is in Libra. Go to the westernmost part of your home (or property, if you prefer to work outdoors).

Carve into a blue candle the rune *Gebu* (also called *Gifu*), which looks like an **X**, and then dress the candle with essential oil of rose, ylang-ylang, jasmine, musk, or patchouli. Use a compass to locate the westernmost spot in your home or on your property and place the candle there. Stand before the candle, facing west, and stare into the flame. Hold your left hand up in front of you, with your palm open to the west, and say: "Gabriel, angel of water, guardian of the west / Please come forth and grant my request."

Let your mind relax, and as you gaze at the flame, gradually see it transform into the figure of Gabriel wearing a blue robe.

Ask the angel to lend divine power and assistance to help you improve your love life. Feel peaceful, loving energy flowing toward you from the west. Ask Gabriel to help you handle a particular romantic problem you are experiencing. When you sense that your request has been granted, thank and release Gabriel. After the angel's shape fades, snuff out the candle.

✡ Rekindle the passion in a relationship.

You'll need:

- a cauldron, hibachi, or barbecue grill
- a lock of your partner's hair
- a lock of your own hair
- a red string or ribbon
- a red envelope
- a pinch of cayenne
- a pinch of paprika
- a pinch of dry mustard
- a pinch of cumin
- a pinch of dried basil
- a pinch of curry powder

Perform this spell outdoors on a Tuesday night when the moon is waxing. Light a fire in your cauldron or barbecue grill. With the red ribbon, tie together the clippings of your hair and your partner's hair, then place them in the envelope. Put the last six ingredients in the envelope and seal it. Drop the envelope in the fire and as it burns, say aloud three times: "As this fire lights up the night / Make my passion and (partner's name) ignite."

✿ Create harmony in a relationship.

You'll need:

- a small shell
- a smooth, small oval or elongated stone
- a stick or cone of rose incense
- a round incense burner or ashtray

Place the stone and the shell in the incense burner or ashtray, along with the incense. The shell symbolizes female energy, the stone represents male energy. Light the incense and let it burn completely. While it burns, ask Venus, Aphrodite, Freya, or another love goddess to promote harmony between you and your partner.

✤ Strengthen a bond between you and a partner.
Cut two pieces of rope, one the same length as your height
and another the same length as your partner's height. Tie the
ropes together in three places along their lengths. Each time
you tie a knot, visualize the bond between you and your partner growing stronger and repeat an affirmation such as:
"(Partner's name) and I pledge ourselves to each other in love,
forsaking all others, now and always." Sprinkle the knotted
ropes with saltwater and then hold them in the smoke of burning incense to charge the spell. Place the ropes under your bed.
(NOTE: Make sure you both really want to be together, for
once formed, this bond is hard to break!)

✿ Drink to your love.

You'll need a chalice, an athame, and either wine or apple cider for this ritual. Pour some wine or cider into the chalice. As the woman holds the chalice, the man should grasp the athame and plunge its blade gently into the chalice. Each person briefly utters a statement or pledge of love for the other, then the man removes the athame and lays it aside. Both partners drink from the chalice to seal their love.

✿ Program a crystal to attract a lover.

Quartz crystals are valued for their ability to amplify the emotional energy you put into them. Wash a crystal to cleanse it of any unwanted vibrations. Hold it to your heart and project loving feelings into it. After a few minutes, hold the crystal to your lips and ask it to bring you a lover who is right for you and will return the feelings of love that you have placed in the crystal. Anoint the crystal with your rosewater potion or special massage oil, then set it in a sunny window where it can transmit your request and draw the right person to you.

✿ End an unwanted relationship.

Perform this spell on a Saturday during the waning moon. With a nail, engrave your name in a white candle. Carve the other person's name in a second white candle. Place them in holders and position them so that the candles are seven inches apart. Tie the two candles together with a piece of string, then light the candles. As they burn, stare into the flames and say aloud three times: "As the fire burns this twine / You go your way and I'll go mine / With peace between us for all time." Cut the string and allow the severed pieces and the candles to burn completely.

✿ Make an astrological love charm.

You'll need:

- your birth chart and your partner's, or a piece of paper and pen
- petals from the flower associated with your sun sign (dried or fresh)
- petals from the flower associated with your partner's
  sun sign (dried or fresh)
- a small piece of your birthstone
- a small piece of your partner's birthstone
- a red or pink pouch, preferably made of silk

If you have birth charts for yourself and your partner, use copies of these in this spell. Otherwise, simply draw a circle in the middle of a piece of paper and sketch the symbols for your sun sign and your partner's sun sign inside the circle. (If you wish, you can add any other images that signify love to you.) In the center of the circle, place the birthstones and flowers. Fold the paper six times, until it is small enough to fit into the pouch. Carry this talisman with you to strengthen your love or give it to your partner.

✵ Cut through an obstacle to your love.

Perform this spell during the waning moon. After centering yourself, bring to mind the problem or obstacle that is standing between you and your partner. In your mind's eye, give this problem a form that you feel represents it vividly—a monster, a wall, whatever you choose. Imagine that you are on one side of this obstacle and your partner is standing on the other side. Hold your athame so that the blade is pointed at the obstacle and slash through the obstacle, moving your dagger back and forth until the obstacle is destroyed. Now that your path is no longer blocked, picture yourself moving toward your partner and embracing, knowing that you have eliminated the problem.

✿ Sever a tie between you and a former lover.

Perform this ritual during the waning moon to break a bond
between you and someone with whom you no longer wish to
be connected. Sit quietly, close your eyes, and imagine you are
seated inside a circle of white light. In your mind's eye, envision your former lover sitting before you in another circle of
white light. Notice a connecting substance that runs from
your heart to the other person's heart, binding you together.
This may look like a beam of light, a rope, a chain, an iron bar,
or something else.

Now, imagine that you are holding a tool that will cut
through this bond—scissors, a knife, a blowtorch, whatever
you need to do the job. Say or think: "I sever this tie and set
us both free / Let there be peace between you and me." In
your mind's eye, slice through the connection, then tie off
both ends of the bond as if it were an umbilical cord. You may
actually feel a twinge as you do this. Envision green light healing the pain of separation. Say good-bye to the other person

and allow his or her image to dissolve, then open your eyes. (NOTE: Perform this ritual as often as necessary until the bond between you is completely broken.)

� Use runes to improve a relationship.

Select *Gebu (Gifu)*, *Wunjo*, and *Kenaz* from a set of runes or paint the symbols on small, round stones. These runes represent love, joy, and passion, respectively. Arrange them in a triangle and place a stick or cone of rose-scented incense in the center of the triangle. Light the incense and ask Venus, Aphrodite, Freya, or another goddess of love to assist you in making your relationship better. Imagine the smoke from the burning incense carrying the energies of these runes into the atmosphere, where they will work to enrich your relationship.

✣ **Let Tui increase the joy in a relationship.**

This hexagram from the *I Ching* signifies joy and harmonious interaction between two people. Cut a circle of pink paper and draw the symbol in the center. Spend a few moments gazing at the hexagram and allowing its message to impress itself on your subconscious. Hang *Tui* in your bedroom, or if you know feng shui, place it in the Relationship Gua of your home. You could also include this symbol in a magical mojo. Or, infuse its pleasant vibrations into a glass of water using the same procedure you followed with a tarot card in Spell 1 for attracting love (see page 75).

✿ Make a locket talisman.

For centuries, lockets have been worn as love talismans and keepsakes. You can enjoy this romantic tradition and strengthen your relationship at the same time. Purchase a heart-shaped locket (silver, copper, or gold). Inside, place a small picture of your lover and one of you (or a photo of the two of you together). Place a bit of your hair and some of your lover's in the locket. Close the locket, anoint it with a drop of your magical massage oil (see page 85), and hang it on a red or pink satiny cord. Pass the locket through the smoke of burning incense (rose, ylang-ylang, patchouli, jasmine, or musk) and repeat this incantation three times: "I love you and you love me / We shall always joyful be." Wear the locket to enhance your love and happiness—each time you touch it, you will be reminded of your intention.

✤ Eat, drink, and be merry.

You'll need:

- two candles (red or pink)
- melted chocolate or ready-made chocolate sauce/topping
- two bowls
- fresh strawberries or raspberries
- a chalice or glass
- apple cider

Certain foods fall into the domain of Venus, goddess (and planet) of love, including apples, chocolate, strawberries, and raspberries. Perform this ritual with a partner to strengthen or celebrate the love between you.

Wash the berries and put them in one bowl. Pour the chocolate into the other bowl. Fill the chalice with cider. Light the candles and sit facing your partner. Dip a berry in the chocolate sauce and feed it to your partner, then ask him or her to feed you. As you do this, say, "May you never hunger." Pass the chalice to your partner and say, "May you never thirst" as he or she drinks. Your partner should then hand you the chalice and repeat the blessing while you drink. Finish the berries and cider; if you wish, you may declare your love or exchange other words of affection in the process.

Chapter 6

Prosperity

Spells

Thursday is ruled by Jupiter, the planet astrologers connect with growth and expansion. If your goal is to increase your income or develop business opportunities, do prosperity magic on a Thursday. However, if you want to stabilize your finances, limit spending, or manage money better, Saturday is a better choice, because Saturn encourages discipline and responsibility. Partnerships fall in Venus's domain, so Friday is a good day to work spells for improving a business partnership or attracting financial backing. People who earn a living in creative fields can also benefit from doing magic on Fridays, as Venus rules the arts, or on Sunday, for the Sun is linked with self-expression.

The moon's phase is important, too. Spells to attract money, enhance investments, improve your public image, or help you get a job or promotion are best performed while the moon is waxing. Plant "seeds" for a new venture just after the new moon. As the moon's light increases, so will whatever you started during this auspicious period. The day of the full moon is a good time to bring projects to fruition or examine how an endeavor is progressing, and if necessary, to make any adjustments.

Pay attention to Mercury's retrograde periods, which occur every four months and last for three weeks at a time. (You'll have to consult an ephemeris, or astrological calendar, for this information.) From our vantage point, the planet appears to be moving backward in its orbit. Investments or ventures begun during this cycle can be problematic—you may not understand all the details, a situation may not turn out the way you'd expected, or an undertaking may might not bear fruit. Because we don't think as clearly while Mercury is retrograde, it usually isn't a good time to work magic; you may overlook something important or get your signals crossed.

When you perform prosperity magic, word your spells carefully to make sure your gain doesn't come at another person's expense. You wouldn't want to get rich because someone died or was injured and you received an insurance settlement! To protect against this, end your affirmations and incantations with a statement such as, "with good to all concerned."

Before you begin a spell or ritual, take a few minutes to relax, center yourself, and clear your mind of any distractions. Envision a ball of white light surrounding you and the space in which you are working, or cast a protective circle according to the method outlined in Chapter 2. Many of the spells in this chapter use candles or fire—handle these with caution and perform your rituals in a safe place.

✡ Make your own money-drawing oil.

This versatile oil can be dabbed on your wrists, added to a magical bath, and used to anoint candles, crystals, gemstones, and talismans. Start with four ounces of almond, grapeseed, or olive oil. Add a few drops of one or more of the following essential oils: peppermint, spearmint, clove, sandalwood, cinnamon, or cedar. When the scent pleases you, add some gold glitter. Pour the oil into a clear or green glass bottle. Affix the label that you make in the following spell to the bottle of oil, making sure the pictures are facing in, against the glass, so they infuse the oil with their power. (NOTE: Some essential oils can be irritating to the skin, so use with care.)

✣ Create a magical prosperity label.

In magic spells, symbols and pictures are often used to influence the subconscious. On a small piece of green paper, draw symbols that represent wealth to you. If you wish, you can also write words, such as *money* or *prosperity*, or an affirmation on the paper. As you work, keep your mind focused on thoughts of obtaining wealth. The finished product can be used as a label for your own custom-blended money-drawing oil (see the previous spell).

✣ Burn a gold candle to attract wealth.

Gold is universally associated with wealth. If you want to attract prosperity into your life, dress a gold candle with peppermint essential oil. On a Thursday when the moon is waxing, light the candle and let it burn down completely. (Make sure to put it in a safe place if you must leave the room.)

✿ **Burn a green candle to increase prosperity.**
Green is the color of healthy, growing plants, and as such, it symbolizes abundance. In some countries, it is also the color of paper money. Carve the word *prosperity* in a green candle. On the day after the new moon, light the candle and let it burn for ten minutes, then snuff it out. Repeat this ritual every day until the full moon or until the candle has completely burned down.

✿ **Burn incense to improve your finances.**
Incense is often burned to send prayers to the deities. Light a stick of mint, clove, or pine incense. While it burns, ask Jupiter, Isis, Fortuna, or another deity to help you improve your fortune. As the smoke rises up to the heavens, it carries your wishes along with it.

✿ Create a wealth sigil.

On a piece of green paper, configure the letters *W, E, A, L, T,* and *H* into a design that you find appealing. The letters can be positioned upright, upside down, backwards, forwards—in any way you like. Use uppercase or lowercase letters, or a combination of both. When you've finished creating your sigil, hang it in a place where you will see it often. Each time you look at it, you'll be reminded of your intention to increase your wealth. If you prefer, you can include your sigil in a magical mojo. (For more about sigils, see Chapter 4.)

✿ Make a botanical prosperity charm.

You'll need:

- a small jar or bottle of clear or green glass
- 3 magnolia blossom petals
- 3 dandelion petals
- 3 geranium petals
- 3 peony petals
- 3 petals from flowers of a plum, peach, or apple tree
- 3 coins (any denominations will work)

Place all the ingredients in the bottle. As you do this, imagine money flowing toward you. Stopper the bottle with a cork, if possible, and seal it with green sealing wax. If this isn't possible, stopper the bottle with green or gold cloth or tissue paper. Place the bottle on a windowsill (preferably in your work area) on the night before the full moon.

✿ Make a spicy prosperity charm.

You'll need:

- 1 stick or cone of pine-scented incense
- a circle of green cloth (preferably silk), 8 inches in diameter
- an 8-inch length of gold ribbon
- a pinch of cinnamon
- a pinch of saffron
- a pinch of rosemary
- a pinch of arrowroot
- a pinch of cardamom
- a pinch of sage
- a pinch of thyme
- a small amount of dried peppermint leaves

Light the incense. Place the last eight ingredients in the center of the circle of cloth. Tie up the cloth with the ribbon, making eight knots. Each time you tie a knot, say or think the words: "My life is now rich with abundance of all kinds." When you have finished, hold the charm in the incense smoke for a few moments to "charge" it. Carry this lucky charm in your pocket to attract prosperity.

✿ Make a magical prosperity mojo.

You'll need:

- a piece of parchment (or good-quality writing paper)
- a pen with green or gold ink
- peppermint or spearmint essential oil
- a small box with a lid (wood, tin, or silver is best)
- a piece of green ribbon
- a piece of gold jewelry
- a small piece of aventurine
- a coin (any denomination)
- an acorn

Write an affirmation, such as, "My life is rich with abundance of all kinds," on the parchment with the green or gold pen. Put a drop of essential oil on the paper and fold it three times. Place the paper in the bottom of the box, then put the last four ingredients in the box. Close the box and tie it with the ribbon. Make eight knots and repeat your affirmation each time you tie a knot. If you wish, you can decorate the box with images, such as dollar signs, that suggest money to you. Carry the mojo in your purse or place it in a desk drawer, cash register, or other spot near where you earn money.

✧ Make a lucky gemstone charm.

You'll need:

- a piece of aventurine (any size will work)
- a piece of turquoise
- a piece of onyx
- a piece of clear quartz
- a piece of jade
- a piece of tigereye
- money-drawing oil
- a green or gold pouch large enough to hold your stones

After you've collected your gemstones, anoint each stone individually with your money-drawing oil (see page 113). As you do this, direct the stones to lend their properties to assist you. Say, "Aventurine, please improve my luck and opportunities," as you rub oil on it. Ask, "Turquoise, will you please bring me good fortune?" as you rub oil on it. Request, "Jade, please increase my practicality and prosperity," as you anoint it. To the piece of tigereye say, "Tigereye, please help me make good decisions." Instruct the onyx to "help me hold on to money." Ask the quartz to "amplify the powers of the other stones." Place each stone in the pouch and keep it with you at all times.

✧ **Wear a carnelian to stimulate career or financial success.**

This reddish orange stone is a powerful motivator. It can help boost your self-confidence, increase your ambition, and spur you to take action toward a goal. Wear a carnelian pendant so that the stone hangs at your heart, where it will bolster your courage. Or wear a ring with a carnelian stone on your index finger to enhance your leadership ability.

✧ **Wear a tigereye to bring good luck in a new job.**

This golden brown stone resembles the glowing eyes of a wild cat. It can help you take control of a situation, improve your judgment and decision-making ability, and attract financial rewards. Wear a tigereye ring on your middle finger to help you clarify goals or strengthen your sense of purpose and commitment. To spark creativity, wear tigereye in a pendant so the stone hangs near your heart.

✵ **Wear aventurine to attract money making opportunities.**

This metallic green stone helps you take advantage of opportunities that come your way. Because it heightens your perception, it is sometimes used to bring good luck in games of chance or when making investments. Wear aventurine in a pendant so that the stone hangs near your solar plexus, where it will stimulate your intuition and help you recognize a good thing when you see it.

✵ **Wear onyx to keep money from slipping away.**

If you have a problem holding on to money, onyx is your stone. Wear this black gemstone in a ring on your middle finger to strengthen your resolve and keep you from spending money too freely. Wear onyx earrings to remind you of your financial priorities. Carry an onyx in your pocket or purse to stabilize your finances.

✿ Take a magical money-drawing bath.

Make yourself a cup of hot peppermint tea while you fill the bathtub with water. Add a few drops of mint, cedar, cinnamon, or pine essential oil to the bathwater. Light a green or gold candle. Play soothing music. The point is to involve all your senses in the process. Soak as long as you like, sipping your herb tea. While you bathe, focus your mind on attracting wealth—you might want to imagine owning luxurious objects or enjoying your prosperity in a number of pleasant ways.

✼ Create a money mandala.

Now that your creative juices are flowing, create a money mandala. *Mandala* means circle in Sanskrit, and this circular image signifies wholeness. Draw a circle, then divide it in half with a horizontal line. The upper portion represents the heavens, the lower half symbolizes earth. Fill both sections with images that signify wealth to you; your picture may be as intricate or simple as you like. While you work, concentrate on attracting prosperity. When you've finished, put a drop of the money-drawing oil you formulated in a previous spell (see page 113) in the center of the mandala. Display your magical mandala where you will see it often.

✿ **Plant seeds to encourage the success of a new financial endeavor.**

On the day after the new moon, place a small piece of clear quartz, a small piece of aventurine, and a coin in a ceramic flowerpot, then fill the pot with soil. Plant seeds for one of the following: parsley, money plant, catnip, daisy, mint, or columbine. These seeds represent the moneymaking venture you are beginning—a new job, project, investment, or other endeavor. Follow the directions on the seed package and tend your seeds with care. As they grow, so will your prosperity.

✿ Insure that you'll never be broke.

Slip a coin of any denomination into a small green or gold pouch, or, if you want to invest more time and energy, make your own green or gold container from cloth, leather, or another material. Sew or pin the pouch inside your wallet or purse. As you do this, say or think: "This coin makes me rich indeed / I have all I want and need." A more elaborate version of this spell involves sewing numerous coins into the hem of a garment, chanting the incantation each time you secure a coin.

✪ Expand your finances.

Jupiter, as mentioned at the beginning of this chapter, is the planet of growth and expansion. Paint the planet's symbol on an ordinary glass jar. Beginning just after the new moon, drop one or more pennies into the jar every day. As you do this, say or think: "This coin now increases itself one hundredfold and brings me prosperity of all kinds." If you know feng shui, place the jar in your Wealth Gua. Otherwise, set it in a prominent spot or in your work area. When the jar is filled, roll the pennies and take them to the bank, then start over.

❋ Program a "money" crystal.

Money crystals contain a mineral in their composition that produces a greenish haze or speckles; some even seem to have chunks of green material growing inside them. After acquiring one, cleanse it by holding it under running water. Anoint it with a few drops of essential oil of peppermint, sandalwood, cedar, clove, or your own money-drawing oil. Hold the crystal to your "third eye" (between your eyebrows) and project images of wealth into it, while you say or think an affirmation such as: "This crystal brings me prosperity of all kinds." Place the crystal on your computer, in your cash drawer, or in your work area. If you know feng shui, set it in your Wealth Gua.

✿ Do a spell to get a job.

You'll need:

- a new one-dollar bill
- money-drawing oil or essential oil of peppermint, clove, or cedar
- a green envelope
- a gold-ink pen

Perform this spell during the waxing moon, at least three days before the full moon (make sure Mercury isn't retrograde at the time). Get a brand new one-dollar bill from the bank: one is the number of new beginnings. Write on the bill an affirmation such as: "I now have the job that is right for me in every way. I am happy, successful, and well paid for my work." Put a drop of money-drawing oil on each corner, then fold the bill three times, repeating your affirmation aloud each time you fold it. Slip the money in the envelope and sleep with it under your pillow until you get your dream job.

✿ Attract prosperity with an *I Ching* hexagram.
The hexagram *Ta Yu* from the ancient Chinese *Book of Changes,*
or *I Ching,* means possession in great measure. Draw this
symbol on a piece of green paper, preferably with a gold-ink
pen, and display it in a prominent place to attract prosperity.
If you wish, you can incorporate this symbol into other spells:
Draw it on a prosperity label or magical mandala, carve it in a
candle, put it in a talisman, or use it to infuse money-drawing
energy into the following potion.

✡ Make a talisman to stabilize your finances.

You'll need:

- a small piece of onyx
- two 3-by-3 inch squares of green cloth
  (silk is best, but cotton or linen will work)
- a sewing needle and black thread
- a 4-by-4-inch square of paper
- dried peppermint or spearmint leaves
- four cloves
- a coin (any denomination)
- a green-ink pen

This is a good spell for people who have trouble holding on to money. Perform it on a Saturday. Write an affirmation such as, "I am prudent with money," or "I buy only what I need," on the paper with the green pen. Repeating your affirmation with each stitch, sew the two squares of green cloth together on three sides. When you've finished, place the mint leaves, the cloves, the onyx, and the coin on the paper, then fold it and slip it into the green pouch you just sewed. Stitch shut the fourth side of the pouch. Carry this talisman in your purse or wallet to help you handle money wisely.

✿ Make a magical money-drawing potion.

On the night before the full moon, brew a cup of peppermint tea. Allow it to cool, then pour it into a green glass bottle. Draw the hexagram *Ta Yu* on a piece of paper and place it on a windowsill, then the set the bottle of tea on the symbol. Allow the moonlight to shine on the bottle overnight, while the symbol's meaning infuses itself into the tea. In the morning, drink the tea and, as you do, visualize yourself as being rich, secure, and happy. Repeat this ritual each month until you have as much money as you need.

✵ Request financial assistance from the north.

You'll need:

- a green pillar candle
- money-drawing oil or essential oil of peppermint
- a nail or pointed implement for carving in the candle
- a piece of aventurine, tigereye, or onyx marked
  with the rune symbol *Daeg* (a black or greenish stone will
  work as a substitute)

North is the direction magicians associate with material and financial matters. The archangel Uriel serves as guardian of the north, so you will be petitioning for his assistance with this ritual. If possible, perform this spell while the moon is in Taurus, Virgo, or Capricorn. If you have a pentagram, wear it during this spell. Carve the rune symbol *Daeg* in the candle, then dress the candle with the money-drawing oil. Place the candle in the northernmost quarter of your home. Set the runestone in front of the candle.

Stand before the candle so that you are facing north, and stare into the flame. Hold your right hand up in front of you, with your palm facing the north, and say: "Uriel, angel of earth, guardian of the north / Please be with me, now come forth." Let your mind relax, and as you gaze at the candle, gradually see it transform into the figure of Uriel wearing a green robe. Ask him to lend his power and assistance to help you improve your financial situation. When you sense he has agreed, thank him and release him. As the angel's shape fades and only the green candle remains, pick up the stone and put it in your pocket as a talisman. Snuff out the candle.

✷ Tap the power of the Part of Fortune.

This symbol looks like a circle with an **X** inside it that divides the circle into four quadrants. In an astrological chart, this auspicious point shows where you will be most fortunate in the material world. You can tap the magical power of this symbol by drawing it on a large sheet of paper, cloth, or other material. You can even sketch it in sand or chalk it on pavement. Step into the center of the Part of Fortune, face east, close your eyes, and take several deep breaths.

As you inhale, feel yourself drawing the energy of the symbol up through your feet until it fills your entire body. Exhale through your mouth quickly, as if you were blowing out candles. As you exhale, send out with your breath a mental announcement that you are open to receiving abundance of all kinds. While staying in the middle of the circle, make a quarter turn so you are facing south, and repeat the announcement and breathing pattern. Do this again, facing west, and finally facing north. Stand in the Part of Fortune for ten minutes each day, or whenever you wish to benefit from its money-drawing power.

✿ Attract money from every direction.

You'll need four coins for this spell (silver dollars are best, but any denomination will work). Anoint each coin with the money-drawing oil you made in an earlier spell (see page 113). Walk to the easternmost point of your property and bury the first coin. If you live in an apartment, bury the coin in a small flowerpot or jar of soil and set it in the easternmost part of your home. Bury the second coin in the south, the third in the west, and the fourth in the north. (NOTE: Be sure to "plant" the coins in this order.) When you have finished, stand at the center of your home or property. Hold your arms out at your sides and spread your feet about eighteen inches apart, so that your body resembles a star. Stand this way for a minute or two while you imagine prosperity flowing toward you from all directions.

✤ Collect money that's owed to you.

This is one of the few spells that should be done while Mercury is retrograde. I've used this spell numerous times and it always works, plus it generates good will between you and the people who owe you money. Write a personal note to your debtors saying that you understand they may be experiencing financial problems, because you feel certain they would have paid you otherwise. Tell them that you are doing a two-part prosperity blessing for them to help them improve their cash-flow situation. The first part goes into effect when they open your note, the second part when you receive the money they owe you. Then actually perform a prosperity spell of your choice for each debtor. This method works much better than angry, threatening calls or letters!

✪ Attract a financial partner or investor.

If possible, perform this spell when the waxing moon is in Libra. You'll need two green or gold candles in candlesticks and something pointed with which to engrave them. Etch your name on one of the candles. Carve appropriate words, such as "financial backer," "investor," or "successful business partner" into the other candle. Dress the candles with money-drawing oil or essential oil of peppermint. Place the candles a foot or so apart and light them. While you let them burn for a few minutes, stare into the flame and envision the right partner or investor coming to you. (NOTE: Don't imagine an actual person—just think of the qualities or resources you seek.) Then snuff out the candles. The next day, move the candles a little closer together and repeat the steps as outlined above. Do this every day until the candles are touching.

✬ Use five tarot cards to attract prosperity.

Choose these five cards from a tarot deck: the ace of pentacles (or coins), the three of pentacles, the nine of pentacles, the ten of pentacles, and the Wheel of Fortune. Pentacles represent money and material considerations. The ace signifies new beginnings and opportunity, the three symbolizes applying your talents for financial gain, the nine stands for rewards you'll receive for your efforts, the ten represents fulfillment and success, and the Wheel of Fortune indicates being in the right place at the right time.

Lay out the cards on the floor in a star formation, then stand in the middle of the star. Close your eyes and feel the prosperity symbolized by the five cards flowing toward you.

✧ Let the Empress help you increase your income.

If your goal is to attract money through a creative endeavor or to be more creative with investments, the Empress card from a tarot deck can help you. The Empress represents the creative, fruitful power of the feminine force. Men as well as women can do this spell, however. The feminine energy you are activating has nothing to do with gender, it is simply one of the two complementary forces operating in the Universe.

Place the card face up on your altar. If you don't have an altar, put the card on a table in the northern section of your home or in the Wealth Gua if you know feng shui. Fill your chalice with water (or use a pretty glass if you don't have a chalice). Set the chalice on top of the card and leave it overnight, so the vibrations of the card infuse into the water.

In the morning, drink the water while you stare at the Empress card. Feel her energy merging with your own, and as you become the Empress, be confident that you can now successfully tackle your money-related goals with creativity, resourcefulness, and imagination. (NOTE: If you don't have a tarot deck, you can use the queen of diamonds from a regular playing deck, but I feel the symbolism of the Empress is more powerful and effective.)

✲ **Let the Emperor help you manage your finances.**
This spell is similar to the previous one, except that your
objective is different. In this case, choose the Emperor card
from a tarot deck, for he symbolizes financial security and
pragmatism. Women as well as men can do this spell; the
masculine energy you are activating has nothing to do with
gender, it is just one of the two complementary forces
operating in the Universe.

Follow the steps outlined in the spell above. When you
drink the energized water, envision yourself becoming the
Emperor and taking on his powers of pragmatism, good
judgment, wise money management, and leadership.
(NOTE: If you don't have a tarot deck, you can use the king
of diamonds from a regular playing deck, but I feel the
symbolism of the Emperor is more powerful and effective.)

✲ Eat your way to financial success.

This spell takes a longer than ten minutes, but it's worth it. Bake a spice cake, using your favorite recipe. The only essential ingredient is cinnamon. As you mix the ingredients together, think about prosperity coming to you. Imagine all the things you'll do with the money you receive. After baking the cake, ice it, and decorate it with symbols that represent prosperity to you, such as dollar signs.

Put one green birthday candle on the cake, light it, make a wish for prosperity, then blow out the candle. Eat a piece of cake every day until it's gone. As you eat the cake, imagine that you are incorporating into yourself all the qualities you need to attract the wealth you desire. If you like, you can invite one or more people to join you in enjoying your money cake—especially if your success involves a partner or other associates.

✡ Dress for success.

Halloween is the Witches' New Year, a time for making plans for the future. That's what dressing up in costumes is really all about—depicting what you want to bring about in the coming year in a very visual and powerful "affirmation." Use this magical technique to attract success and abundance by dressing as you would if you were as accomplished and wealthy as you desire. When you put on these garments, envision yourself as being successful, rich, and happy.

✡ Give something back.

Magicians believe that there is no limit to the abundance in the Universe, and that there is plenty for everyone. You needn't worry that by increasing your fortune you will decrease someone else's. However, you can help keep the cycle of prosperity turning, and thereby generate more for yourself, by giving back a portion of everything you receive. Some people call this "seed money," for you are indeed planting seeds that will mature in the future and return benefits to you, like any sound investment will. When your prosperity spells generate income, share a percentage with a charity or someone else who needs it. As you do this, envision ten times the amount you give away returning to you. The old saying "What goes around, comes around" holds true in magic!

Chapter 7

Spells for Protection, Health, and Well-Being

Centuries ago, wise men and women used their knowledge of magic, herbalism, nature, and the cosmos in the practice of healing. Recently, the renewed interest in holistic medicine has led us to once again explore the mind-body dynamics that influence health. Although magic isn't a substitute for professional medical care, it can aid the healing process and contribute to your overall sense of well-being.

Lunar cycles, in particular, affect mental, emotional, and physical conditions. More babies are born during the full moon, and patients in mental hospitals often exhibit more extreme behavior at this time. Many people feel more energetic during the full moon and experience decreased vitality around the time of the new moon. Therefore, you'll want to pay close attention to the moon's position when doing magic intended to impact health and safety. Spells designed to promote growth, such as the formation of new tissue after an injury, should be performed during the waxing moon. Spells that encourage diminution—weight loss or slowing a disease's progression, for instance—are more effective if done during the waning moon.

Saturday, which is "Saturn's day," is the best time to perform most protection rituals and spells because Saturn is the planet associated with boundaries, stability, and structure. Unless otherwise noted, perform the protection spells in this chapter on a Saturday. Saturday is also a good day to do magic that involves an ending or letting go, such as giving up a bad habit, as well as spells to bind an enemy, keep an illness from spreading, or strengthen your determination.

Thursday, which is governed by Jupiter, favors spells that involve increase or expansion. If, for example, you want to boost your stamina, perform magic on a Thursday when the moon is waxing. Because Jupiter also rules long-distance travel, Thursday is the best day to do magic for safe journeys. Sunday, the "Sun's day," supports spells that enhance vitality, confidence, and general well-being.

Some of the spells and rituals in this chapter, like those in the previous chapters, include the use of candles and fire. Once again, safety and common sense precautions should be exercised to prevent accidents. Perform these spells in safe places designed for such things (woodstoves, fireplaces, barbecue grills), and don't leave burning candles unattended.

✡ Protect yourself with white light.

Don't be misled by the simplicity of this quick and easy
spell—it is very effective. Whenever you feel the need for a
little extra protection, relax, close your eyes, and imagine that
you are completely surrounded by a cocoon of pure white
light. As you do this, repeat this affirmation three times:
"I am protected by white light. Nothing can harm me."

✿ Protect someone else with white light.

You can also use this protection spell to keep someone else safe. Calm yourself, clear your mind, then imagine the person you want to protect. Next, envision that person enclosed in a cocoon of pure white light. Repeat this affirmation three times: "(Name of person) is protected by white light. Nothing can harm (him/her)." The spell works for pets, too.

✪ Protect your home with basil.

Fill a large pot with water and add a bunch of fresh basil.
Bring the water to a boil, then let the basil steep in it for a
few minutes. Remove the basil and spread it on a towel to dry.
(Save it to use in other spells.) After the water has cooled,
pour it on your doorsteps to keep intruders (human or otherwise) from entering your home. If you wish, you can pour a
circle of basil-infused water around the outside of your home.

✿ Protect your home with a rowan wreath.

The rowan tree, sometimes called European mountain ash in America, is thought to possess strong protective powers. Hang a wreath or other decoration made of rowan on your door to protect your home. If rowan isn't available in your area, hang a wreath made with ash or pussy willow on your door instead.

✿ Plant flowers to protect your home.

White is the color of protection, so you can create a protective barrier around your home by planting white flowers between your house and the street, in window boxes, on either side of your front door—wherever your needs and taste dictate. Peonies and snapdragons are two of the best-loved protection botanicals. Plant these near your home to keep it safe.

✿ Plant a protective herb garden.

Many of the herbs and spices associated with Italian cooking can also help protect your home. To enhance safety, plant an herb garden with basil, fennel, garlic, and/or anise.

✿ Draw a circle of safety.

On a large sheet of white paper or cardboard, use a black marker to draw a circle big enough for you to stand in. You can draw a pentagram or write *Safe Zone* inside the circle if you wish. Whenever you need to, you can step inside this circle of safety. To intensify your protection, imagine a column of white light enveloping you as it shines upward from the circle.

✡ Make your own magical protection oil.

Start with five ounces of olive, grapeseed, or almond oil. Add a few drops of essential oil of fennel, basil, and/or verbena. Drop a small piece of amber into the oil, then pour your mixture into an amber-colored glass bottle. Draw a pentagram on the bottle and say aloud: "This magical oil keeps me safe at all times and in all situations." You can use your protection oil to anoint candles, crystals and gemstones, amulets, or apply it directly to your skin (see the spell on the next page).

✿ Draw a pentagram with protection oil.

Stand inside your circle of safety. Shake your bottle of protection oil three times, then put a dab of the oil on your index finger. Use the oil to draw a pentagram on your forehead, in the spot between your eyebrows known as the "third eye," and make a circle around the pentagram. Do this anytime you feel a need for some extra protection — it's also a good way to begin a magic ritual. (NOTE: Some people are sensitive to essential oils, so use them with care.)

✵ Use salt to purify your home.

To cleanse your home of unwanted energies, sprinkle a little sea salt in the corners of each room. This is a good way to dispel the former occupants' vibrations when you move into a new residence. You can also perform this spell after an argument or other disruptive experience.

✤ Burn sage to smudge your home.

Burning white sage is a traditional method for purifying a space. To remove unwanted vibrations from your home (or any other area), light a bundle of sage or sage incense and let the smoke waft through each room. The smoke "smudges" the space and clears it of all unbalanced or inharmonious energies.

✿ Sweep away unwanted energies.

Many people think witches ride broomsticks, but they're mistaken. A broom's real magical purpose is to clear a space of harmful, disruptive, or unbalanced energies in preparation for a ritual or other spellworking. You can use a regular, everyday broom for this purpose or, if you're so inclined, make your own ritual broom from straw, cornhusks, and other natural materials. Before you cast a circle or perform a magic spell, literally sweep the air where you'll be working to remove any unwanted vibrations.

✡ Use your athame to slice through unwanted energies.

The athame or magical dagger is primarily a banishing tool, used to remove unwanted energies. Perform this ritual when you first move into a new place, after an argument or other disturbance, before doing a magic ritual, and whenever you feel a need to "clear the air." Hold your athame before you, with your arm outstretched, and sweep it from side to side, as if you were cutting through vegetation in a forest. While you're doing this, say aloud: "This space is now cleared of all harmful, disruptive, unbalanced energies." As you banish the dark cloud of negativity, envision pure, white light filling the space around you.

✡ Make an herbal protection amulet.

You'll need:

- 1 stick or cone of incense (amber-scented is best)
- a circle of white cloth (preferably silk), 9 inches in diameter
- a 9-inch length of black ribbon
- a basil leaf or a pinch of dried basil
- a bit of ash, rowan, or pussy willow bark
- a small clove of garlic
- a few fennel seeds
- a piece of star anise
- a few snapdragon petals (white, if possible)
- peony seeds or petals (white, if possible)

Light the incense. Place the last seven ingredients in the center of the circle of cloth. Tie up the cloth with the ribbon, making nine knots. Each time you tie a knot, say or think the words: "I am (or someone else is) protected at all times and in all situations." When you have finished, hold the amulet in the incense smoke for a few moments to "charge" it. Carry this protection amulet with you to keep you safe, or give it to someone else who needs a little extra protection.

✤ **Draw a sigil to keep you safe while traveling.**

On a piece of white paper, configure the letters *S, A, F, E, T,* and *Y* into a design that you find appealing. The letters can be written upright, upside down, backwards, normally—in any way you choose. Use uppercase or lowercase letters, printed or script, or a combination. Draw a circle around the design you've created. When you've finished, fold your sigil three times. Carry it with you whenever you travel. If you prefer, you may place it in the glove compartment of your car to provide protection. Or, include your sigil in a protection amulet. (For more about sigils, see chapter 4.)

✡ Program a crystal to protect you.

Quartz crystals are prized for their ability to "remember."
You can program a crystal to keep you or someone else safe.
First, cleanse the crystal by holding it under running water
(see chapter 4). Next, place the crystal against your forehead
and project this affirmation into the crystal: "This crystal
keeps me safe at all times and in all situations." If you prefer,
you can hold the crystal to your lips and say the affirmation
aloud. Carry the crystal with you whenever you want to have a
little extra protection. If you wish, you can include this spe-
cially programmed crystal in a magical mojo (see the following spell).

✿ Make a magical protection mojo.

You'll need:

- a piece of white parchment (or good-quality writing paper)
- a black-ink pen
- basil essential oil
- a small white box with a lid
- a piece of black ribbon
- a small piece of amber
- a small piece of clear quartz crystal
- a piece of ash bark or an ash leaf
- a pinch of fennel
- a small silver pentagram or star (or draw a pentagram in silver ink on the parchment)

With the black pen, write an affirmation, such as, "I am safe at all times and in all situations" on the parchment. Put a drop of essential oil on it and fold it three times. Place the paper in the bottom of the box, then put the last five ingredients in the box. Close the box and tie it with the ribbon. Make nine knots and repeat your affirmation as you tie each knot. Draw pentagrams (five-pointed stars) on the box. Carry the mojo with you during the day and put it under your bed at night. If you wish, you can keep it in the glove compartment of your car or in your workplace—anywhere you feel the need for a little extra protection.

✪ Create a safe space.

This ritual can be performed as a preliminary to doing magical work. It can also be used to protect yourself, another person, your home, or any area you choose. Use your imagination to make the circle as large as you need it to be for your purposes.

Face east and extend your right arm in front of you. With your finger (or your wand or athame, if you prefer) draw a pentagram in the air in front of you. Imagine the pentagram glowing bluish-white in front of you. With your arm still extended, turn ninety degrees in a clockwise direction, until you are facing south. You have just drawn an arc of bluish-white light connecting these two points. Now, draw another pentagram in the air and see it glowing bluish white. Again, turn ninety degrees, drawing an arc of light with your hand or tool. When you are facing west, draw another pentagram. Turn ninety degrees, and when you are facing north, draw another pentagram. Turn until you face east again and have drawn a complete circle in the air before you. Lower your arm and say,

"This circle is now cast. Everything within this circle is safe from all harm."

When you are finished with your spell or ritual, open the circle again. Start at the east, extend your arm, and begin turning counterclockwise. As you turn, imagine you are removing the protective barrier of light that you cast earlier. When you arrive back at the east, lower your arm and say, "The circle is open, but unbroken."

✿ Wear amber for protection.

Amber possesses great protective powers. Wear amber jewelry, carry a piece of amber in your pocket, or rub soft amber resin on your skin to keep you safe from harm.

I know an Italian woman who rescued many people during the Bosnian war. Each time she entered that turbulent country, she wore an amber necklace, earrings, and bracelets. Neither she nor any of the people she helped to escape during her numerous trips were hurt.

✿ Get help from the four archangels.

According to mystical and magical traditions, each of the four archangels—Raphael, Gabriel, Michael, and Uriel—presides over one of the four directions. You can elicit their help and protection by enacting this ritual. This technique can also be combined with the previous ritual if you wish to invite them to participate in other spells and practices.

Face east and envision the archangel Raphael standing before you. Say aloud: "Before me, Raphael, angel of air, guardian of the east, please guide and protect me." Next, imagine Gabriel standing behind you and say: "Behind me, Gabriel, angel of water, guardian of the west, please guide and protect me." Now visualize Michael to your right and say: "To my right, Michael, angel of fire, guardian of the south, please guide and protect me." Finally, imagine Uriel on your left as you say: "To my left, Uriel, angel of earth, guardian of the north, please guide and protect me."

✿ Burn a white candle for protection.

With a nail or other sharp implement, carve the word *protection* in a white candle. Dress the candle with essential oil of basil or amber. Light the candle and let it burn for ten minutes, then snuff it out. Do this each day for ten minutes until the candle has burned completely.

✿ Burn a candle to protect someone else.

With a nail or other sharp implement, carve the word *protection* on one side of a white candle and the name of the person you wish to protect on the other side. Dress the candle with essential oil of basil or amber. Tie around the candle a lock of the person's hair or a strip of cloth from clothing he or she has worn. Light the candle and let it burn for ten minutes, then snuff it out. Do this each day for ten minutes until the candle has burned completely. Allow the hair or cloth to burn, too.

✷ Burn a black candle to banish negativity.

This is a good spell to perform if you are bothered by another person's negativity. With a nail or other sharp implement, carve the word *banish* on a black candle, along with the name of the person whose energy you wish to deflect. Light the candle and stare into the flame while you say the words: "Whatever (name of the person) sends to me returns to (him/her) immediately." Let the candle burn for ten minutes, then snuff it out. Do this each day for ten minutes until the candle has burned completely.

✧ Burn a green candle for good health.

With a nail or other sharp implement, carve the word *health* in a green candle. Though it isn't necessary, you may want to dress the candle with the essential oil that relates to the condition you wish to heal (refer to a good book on essential oils, such as *The Art of Aromatherapy*, by Robert B. Tisserand). Light the candle and let it burn for ten minutes, then snuff it out. Do this each day until the candle has burned completely.

If you are doing this spell for someone else, carve that person's name in the candle, too. Tie around the candle a lock of hair or a piece of cloth from a garment he or she has worn. Make sure to ask this person's permission before you perform this healing spell.

✿ Burn a blue candle to relieve stress.

With a nail or other sharp implement, etch the word *calm* on a blue candle. Dress the candle with essential oil of lavender. Light the candle and let it burn for ten minutes while you sit quietly and gaze into the flame. Breathe slowly and deeply, enjoy the soothing scent of lavender. Snuff the candle out after ten minutes. Do this each day until the candle has burned completely or until you no longer feel stressed out.

✪ Make a personal seal of protection.

Think of your personal seal as a symbolic shield that protects you from all harm. You can draw it on paper, or if you want to invest more time and effort in it, embroider it on fabric, carve it on wood, engrave it in metal—be creative. It's best to start with a copy of your birth chart for this special amulet, but if you don't have one (and don't want to wait to have one calculated for you), sketch the symbol for your zodiac sign and write your birth date below it, then draw one circle around both items. Write your full name around the inside edge of the circle. Add any other protection images you wish: your totem animal, a pentagram, a guardian angel, sigils, lucky numbers, et cetera. Display your personal seal on the inside of your home's front door or carry it with you to keep you safe.

✸ Protect yourself with a blue star.

Stand with your legs about a foot apart. Hold your arms straight out at your sides, so that your body forms a star. Close your eyes, take a few deep breaths, and relax. Starting with your left foot, envision a line of blue light running up the front of your leg to the top of your head, then down your body again to your right foot. Continue mentally drawing this blue light up and across your body and out to your left hand. Next, imagine the blue light crossing your chest and running out to your right hand. Finally, envision the line of blue light flowing down your left leg to your foot. You have now super-imposed a blue star or pentagram over your body, where it will act as a shield to protect you against harm.

✵ Wear a pentagram for protection.

Five-pointed stars or pentagrams are symbols of protection and witches, in particular, often wear them for this reason. (The star-shaped badges sheriffs in the Wild West used to wear served the same purpose.) You can purchase a pentagram in a new-age store or online. Wear it in good health!

✵ Draw a pentagram on your body.

If you don't want to wear a piece of jewelry in the shape of a pentagram or if you need protection quickly and don't have one with you, you can draw a pentagram on your body. With a washable marker (one that's OK to use on skin), draw a five-pointed star over your heart to keep you safe.

✡ Use green light to heal a cut.

Green is the color of growth and it can help promote the growth of healthy new tissue. Close your eyes and envision bright green light surrounding the injured tissue. Imagine the green light sealing up the cut and gradually erasing it. In your mind's eye, see new skin replacing the damaged skin until the wound is completely healed. Do this visualization for ten minutes each day (or several times a day) until the cut is healed. (NOTE: You can do this magic spell for someone else, too, but remember to ask that person's permission, first.)

✿ Use magic thread to help a broken bone heal faster.

This spell, much like the previous one, promotes healing and the growth of new tissue. After a broken bone has been profession-ally set, imagine yourself stitching the two pieces back together with magic thread made of green light. As you perform this task, see the bone becoming strong, whole, and healthy again. The more vividly you can picture this in your mind's eye, the better. Spend ten minutes each day (or more if you wish) sewing the bone back together until it is completely healed.

✿ Burn up an unwanted habit.

If you want to be rid of an old habit or behavior that is interfering with your health or well-being, this spell can help. During the waning moon, write on a piece of paper the habit you wish to release. Hold the paper over a cauldron, pot, sink, barbecue grill, or other fireproof receptacle. Light the paper and let it burn while you repeat this affirmation: "I no longer want or need (tobacco, alcohol, caffeine, or whatever) and release all attachment to it." Drop the burning paper into the receptacle before the flames reach your fingers! As you watch the paper burn, feel your attachment to the habit dissolving. Do this each night (if necessary) until the moon is new, then stop. If you still haven't kicked your habit, perform the spell again on each night between the next full moon and the next new moon until you are free of the behavior.

✡ Make a magical stress-release potion.

You'll need:

- a piece of light blue paper
- a darker blue pen
- lavender essential oil
- chamomile tea
- a glass bottle
- sea salt

Perform this spell on the night of the new moon. On the piece of paper, draw a symbol that represents peace and relaxation to you, or create a sigil using the letters from a word such as *calm, peace, tranquility,* or *serenity.* Brew a cup of chamomile tea (chamomile is known for its soothing properties). Allow the tea to cool, then pour it into the bottle. Add a few drops of lavender essential oil and a teaspoon of sea salt. Place the drawing on a windowsill and set the bottle on top of your drawing, where it will catch the vibrations emanating from the "dark moon." Leave it overnight to allow the drawing's meaning to infuse itself into the liquid in the bottle. In the morning, your magic potion is ready to pour into a hot, relaxing bath.

✡ Mark the four directions to protect your property.

You can use this ritual to protect your property. Gather four rocks, each about the size of your hand. Paint a yellow pentagram on one, a blue pentagram on another, a green one on the third, and a red one on the fourth. Use a compass to locate the easternmost point on your property, then place the rock with the yellow pentagram there. Put the red-marked rock at the southernmost point. Place the blue one in the west and the green one in the north. These rocks create an energy barrier around your property that will protect it from harm.

✡ Use a "circle" rock to provide protection.

During their formation, rocks may incorporate more than one type of material in their composition. In some cases, a band or circle of a different color naturally results. Magicians prize these "circle" rocks because the circle is an ancient symbol of protection and wholeness, giving the rocks special protective power. If you find a rock with an unbroken band around it, pick it up and carry it with you to keep yourself safe. Put it in the glove compartment of your car or in your suitcase to protect yourself while traveling.

Large circle rocks make ideal "guardians" for your home. Set one on either side of your front door or at the entrance to your property to deter intruders or unwanted solicitors. If you prefer, place a large circle rock at each of the four corners of your home, business, or yard or mark the four directions with them to create a protective circle around your property.

✿ Use quartz crystals to protect your property.

You'll need lots of small, inexpensive quartz crystals for this spell—the number depends on the size of your property. Place all the crystals in a colander or large sieve and cleanse them of any unwanted energies by holding them under running water (tap water will work fine if you don't have a stream nearby). Hold your hand over the collection of crystals and envision them filled with protective white light as you say or think: "These crystals protect my property and keep it safe at all times, in all situations."

With a trowel or large spoon, dig a hole at each corner of your property and set one crystal in each hole. Next, bury a crystal at each of the four directions. Bury several more crystals between these points to form a secret, magical barrier around your property. When you've finished, stand at the center of the property and visualize the buried crystals emitting powerful vibrations, rather like an electrified fence, that prevent intruders from entering.

✸ Make a magic charm to protect a pet.

You'll need:

- a small receptacle to attach to your pet's collar
- a piece of white paper
- a pen with black ink
- amber resin or a small chunk of amber
- a pinch of basil
- a bit of ash bark or leaf

To hold these ingredients, use a leather pouch, a circular silver locket, or any other small container that can be attached to your pet's collar—the choice depends on your pet's size and your preference. Use the pen and paper to create a sigil from the letters in your pet's name, as described in Chapter 4. Draw a protective circle around the sigil, then rub the opposite side of the paper with amber resin or tape a piece of amber at the center of your drawing of the sigil. Lay the basil and bit of ash on the paper, fold these ingredients up in the paper until the packet is small enough to fit into the container, and slip the tiny packet into the container. Affix the charm to your pet's collar as you visualize him or her surrounded by a cocoon of white light.

✡ Make yourself invisible.

You'll need:

- a black candle
- a circle of black cloth (silk is best)
- fern seeds
- a small piece of snowflake obsidian, black tourmaline, or smoky quartz crystal
- black string, cord, or thread

This spell won't actually make you disappear, it merely prevents other people from seeing you if you don't want them to. Use fern seeds collected just before midnight on the day during which the summer solstice occurred. (NOTE: you should do this annually to ensure that you'll have them when you need them.) Perform this spell on the night of the new moon. Light the candle. Place the seeds in the circle of black cloth, along with the stone. Tie the circle closed with the cord, making seven knots. With each knot, say or think this incantation: "I am free / to come and go / Magic shields me / None will know." Allow the candle to burn down completely, or, if this isn't possible, let it burn for ten minutes and then snuff it out. Stare into the flame and envision yourself surrounded by a cloak of darkness that keeps anyone from seeing you as you go about your business in complete secrecy.

✿ Protect yourself while flying.

Birds are at home in the air, so you can use them as "totem" animals to protect you the next time you fly. Collect several feathers; they can all be from the same or different kinds of birds. On a piece of white ribbon, write the words "safe journey." Tie the feathers together with the ribbon. If you want to get creative, attach gemstones, decorative beads, or tiny charms (such as angels, totem animals, gods and goddesses, or other guardian figures) to the ribbon or the feathers. Light a stick of incense and hold the bundle of feathers in the smoke (representing the element of air) while you envision yourself flying safely to your destination. Fasten the feather charm to your carry-on bag.

✡ Let a magic word keep you safe.

You've probably heard the magic word *abracadabra*, but don't know what it means. This word of power is actually a combination of gods' names, and when you speak or write it, you invoke the blessings of those deities and ward off evil. Make a protection amulet by writing the magic word in the shape of a triangle. Display it in your home, workplace, car—wherever you wish to promote safety and well-being.

```
          A
         AB
         ABR
        ABRA
        ABRAC
       ABRACA
       ABRACAD
      ABRACADA
      ABRACADAB
     ABRACADABR
    ABRACADABRA
```

✣ **Balance your chakras to promote good health.**

The "chakras" are energy vortices in the body, according to spiritual and healing traditions in the East. (*Chakra* means wheel in Sanskrit.) When these energy centers are open and balanced, you enjoy good health, but when they become blocked, physical and/or emotional problems can occur. The seven main chakras run from the base of your spine to the top of your head. The first, or "root," chakra is located at the base of the spine, the second lies a few inches below your belly button, the third is at your solar plexus, the fourth is near your heart, the fifth lies between your collarbones at the base of your throat, the sixth is in the region of the "third eye" between your eyebrows, and the seventh is at the crown of your head.

To activate these chakras and keep your vital energy flowing smoothly through this channel and to all parts of your body, sit quietly for ten minutes each day and focus colored light on these centers, one at a time, from the lowest to the highest. Imagine red light warming the root chakra. Envision orange light filling your lower abdomen. See yellow light glowing in your solar plexus. Visualize green light around your heart. Imagine blue light at the base of your throat. Focus indigo light between your eyebrows. Envision purple light at the top of your head.

✿ Use pyramid protection against psychic attack.

This spell sounds simple, but that doesn't mean it won't very effectively repel "bad vibes." If you feel that someone is sending harmful thoughts and energy your way, face the direction from which the "attack" is coming. Form a triangle with your fingers, with the tips of your index fingers and thumbs touching each other. Hold your hands up to your forehead so that your thumbs "underline" your eyebrows, your fingers point upward, and your "third eye" falls within the triangle. Close your eyes and take a deep breath. As you exhale, use your hands to physically push the unwanted vibrations back in the direction they came from. (You may want to follow up this spell with another one in this chapter to provide additional protection.)

✢ Invoke the aid of your personal guardian.

Many people sense the presence of their personal guardians
and relate amazing stories of how these nonphysical beings
have helped them in times of need. Whether you think of
these entities as angels, spirit guides, totem animals, gods and
goddesses, or ancestors, they are here to help and protect you.
You can invoke your guardian and avail yourself of its assistance whenever you wish—all you have to do is call. If you
already feel a connection to your guide or guardian, create a
special call or chant to request its assistance. Here's an example: "Guardian angel, ever near / Now I seek your presence
here / Come, angel, come." Envision your guardian standing
near you, shielding you from harm or lending you its power to
handle the challenge facing you. If you haven't yet experienced
your guardian's presence in your life, spend some time medi-
tating in order to make its acquaintance and strengthen the
link between you. In time, your guardian will make itself
known to you.

Chapter 8

Spells to Bring Good Luck and Happiness

Most people believe that "good luck" is a matter of fate or chance. But magicians know that we make our own luck. By intentionally directing our thoughts, emotions, and willpower toward our objectives, we can consciously create the circumstances we desire.

Astrologers connect Jupiter with luck, so it's usually best to work spells designed to attract good fortune—especially if they involve travel or expansion of some kind—on Jupiter's day, Thursday. If your spell includes another person, such as a romantic or business partner, you may wish to tap the energy of Venus and do your magic on Friday. Sunday favors creative endeavors and spells to enhance personal power, confidence, or image.

Perform spells and rituals that promote growth during the waxing moon. If your goal is to decrease or end something, do your magic while the moon is waning. Coordinate spells for initiating new beginnings with the new moon, and spells that bring matters to a conclusion with the full moon.

Before you do the spells in this chapter, take a few minutes to relax, center yourself, and clear your mind of any distractions. To ensure your protection, envision a ball of white light surrounding you and the space you're working in, or cast a circle according to the method outlined in Chapter 2. If you are using candles or fire, remember to take common sense safety precautions to avoid accidents and injury.

✿ Use magic to find a parking space.

This easy spell can save you lots of time and aggravation. Shortly before you reach your destination, clearly envision the place you are visiting and imagine an empty parking space nearby. (NOTE: Don't visualize someone pulling out of a space, simply see the vacant spot waiting for you.)

✲ Charge water to bring good luck.

If you have a magical chalice, use it for this spell. Otherwise, a regular glass will do. Perform this spell on the night of the full moon. Place a small piece of jade in the glass, then fill the glass with water and set it down. Hold your hands on either side of the glass, but don't actually touch it. Close your eyes and imagine golden light flowing between your hands. This golden light represents good luck. The light runs right through the glass of water, making the water glow and the piece of jade sparkle. Hold this image in your mind for a minute or so, until you sense that the water has taken the charge. Leave the glass sitting in the moonlight overnight. The next morning, remove the jade and drink the water, letting its magical energy fill you with good luck.

✡ Wear gold to spark creativity.

Gold is ruled by the sun, the heavenly body that astrologers associate with creativity and self-expression. Wearing gold jewelry brings the sun's energy into your personal sphere, enabling you to draw on its creative vibrations for your own purposes.

✡ Wear gold for courage and leadership.

Throughout history, gold has been considered a precious metal of great value. Kings and queens wear crowns made of gold. The alchemists worked magic to turn lead into gold. Ruled by the sun, the center of our solar system, gold contains vibrations that can enhance your own courage, self-esteem, and leadership ability. Wear it whenever you need to feel stronger, more confident, important, or powerful.

✡ Wear silver to balance emotions and improve intuition.

Silver falls into the moon's domain, and astrologers connect the moon with the emotions, intuition, and comfort. Wearing silver jewelry or carrying a silver talisman can help you balance your emotions so that you feel more secure, peaceful, and comfortable. Silver can also improve your interactions with other people, especially family members and loved ones. If you want to strengthen your intuition, silver is your metal; combine it with amethyst, moonstone, pearl, or aquamarine for the best results.

✿ Create an affirmation for happiness.

Repeating an affirmation, chant, prayer, incantation, or other positive statement sends vibrations out into the Universe to create the circumstances you desire. Design a short affirmation for happiness and well-being, such as: "I am in harmony with Divine Will and at one with the Universe, and all is well," or "Happiness and good fortune of all kinds are mine now." Say this aloud at least ten times each day to stimulate blessings in your life. If you wish, you can also write your affirmation on a piece of paper and display someplace where you will see it often. Or, incorporate the written affirmation into a magical good luck charm.

✩ Use amethyst to bring pleasant dreams.

Amethysts influence the unconscious mind and promote serenity, emotional healing, and psychic awareness. Wear them to
help overcome sleep problems, especially those caused by nervous
tension or fear of the unknown. Place an amethyst under your
pillow at night to encourage pleasant dreams and restful sleep.
You can also include a small piece of amethyst in a magical
mojo to promote peace of mind and emotional calm.

✼ Burn incense to attract good luck.

Incense is often burned to send prayers to the deities. Light a
stick of sandalwood-, myrrh-, cedar-, frankincense-, bergamot-,
lemongrass-, or orange-scented incense. While it burns, ask
Jupiter, Thor, Isis, Fortuna, Brigid, or another deity to help
you attract good fortune. Say aloud an affirmation such as, "I
am open and receptive to all good." As the smoke rises up to
the heavens, it carries your requests along with it.

✿ Make a spicy good-luck charm.

You'll need:

- a stick or cone of sandalwood-, cedar-, or myrrh-scented incense
- a circle of orange cloth (preferably silk), 9 inches in diameter
- a 9-inch length of yellow or gold ribbon
- a pinch of alfalfa
- a pinch of sage
- a pinch of cardamom
- a pinch of arrowroot
- a pinch of celery seed
- a small amount of dried oak leaf or bark

Light the incense. Place the last six ingredients in the center of the circle of cloth. Tie up the cloth with the ribbon, making nine knots. Each time you tie a knot, say or think the words: "My life is now rich with good fortune, joy, and blessings of all kinds." When you have finished, hold the charm in the incense smoke for a few moments. Carry the charm in your pocket to attract good luck.

✣ Make a botanical good luck charm.

You'll need:

- a jar or bottle made of clear or amber glass
- 9 acorns
- 9 dandelion, sunflower, or marigold petals
- 9 chamomile buds
- 9 peony seeds
- 9 violet petals
- 3 small pieces of jade
- 3 small pieces of tigereye
- 3 small pieces of malachite

Place all the ingredients in the bottle. As you do this, keep positive thoughts in your mind to help you attract good fortune of all kinds. Stopper the bottle with a cork, if possible, and seal it with yellow or golden sealing wax. If this isn't possible, stopper the bottle with yellow or golden cloth or tissue paper. Place the bottle in your bedroom window on the night before the full moon. Afterward, display it on your altar or in another prominent spot.

✣ Make a lucky mojo.

You'll need:

- a piece of parchment (or good-quality writing paper)
- a pen with orange or gold ink
- sweet orange, bergamot, cedar, or sandalwood essential oil
- a small box with a lid (wood or tin is best)
- a piece of orange or gold ribbon
- a small gold bead or piece of gold jewelry
- a small piece of malachite
- a piece of coral
- a piece of clear quartz crystal

Write an affirmation, such as, "Good fortune comes to me from all directions," on the parchment in orange ink. Put a drop of essential oil on it and fold it three times. Place the paper in the bottom of the box, then put the last four ingredients in the box. Close the box and tie it with the ribbon. Make nine knots and repeat your affirmation each time you tie a knot. If you wish, you can decorate the box with images of, for example, four-leaf clovers or rainbows—things that suggest luck to you. Store the mojo in a safe place.

✪ Draw positive energy from the four directions.

You'll need a bell for this ritual. After centering yourself and casting a circle according to the instructions in Chapter 2, face east and point your magic wand, athame, or index finger (if you don't have a wand or athame) in that direction. Ask the guardians of the east to help you improve your mental abilities and communication skills. Envision this power flowing from the east, through your wand or athame, and into your body.

Ring the bell, then turn clockwise to face south. Ask the guardians of the south to strengthen your creativity, vitality, and enthusiasm. Feel these qualities streaming toward you from the south. Ring the bell, then turn to face west. Ask the guardians of the west to balance your emotions and improve your relationships with other people. Feel help flowing to you from the west, then ring the bell and turn toward the north. Ask the guardians of the north to assist you with your finances and other practical matters. Feel aid coming to you from this direction, then ring the bell. Turn again to face the east. Lower your arm and stand in the center of the circle for a few minutes, absorbing the positive energy coming to you from all directions. When you are ready, thank the four guardians and open the circle according to the instructions in Chapter 2.

✿ Light candles at the four directions.

This ritual is similar to the previous one and draws upon the positive forces of the four compass points to enhance your happiness and good fortune. You'll need four votive candles—one red, one blue, one green, and one yellow—and containers to hold them safely. Place the yellow candle at the easternmost point of your property or room and light it. Take a moment to absorb the positive energy generated here. Walk clockwise and set the red candle in the south. Light it and feel the beneficial energy radiating from this point. Walk clockwise to the west, place the blue candle there, and light it, drawing in the good vibrations from this direction. Walk clockwise to the north, set the green candle there and light it, basking in the lucky energy at this spot. When you've finished, move to the center of the circle you've created. Imagine positive energy and good fortune flowing from all directions toward you, bringing you whatever you desire. If you want, you can make a wish or request at this time. When you're ready, snuff out the yellow candle, then move in a counterclockwise direction around the circle, snuffing out each candle in turn.

✹ Program a crystal to bring you luck.

Quartz crystals can be programmed with an intention and, once programmed, you can carry them with you, place them in a prominent spot in your home, or add them to other magical charms. Wash your crystal under running water to cleanse it of unwanted vibrations. Form an image or affirmation in your mind that describes something you desire—or simply request good luck and happiness. While thinking about your wish, hold the crystal to your lips and blow gently on it to infuse it with your intention.

✿ Give your problems to a smoky quartz crystal.

Magicians prize smoky quartz for its ability to store emotions and thoughts for long periods. These crystals process material very slowly, so they can keep something "on ice" until you are ready to deal with it. If you are experiencing a problem, particularly one of an emotional nature, you can give it to a smoky quartz crystal to hold temporarily. Press the crystal to your heart and release the disturbing feelings into it. As you feel your load lightening and the emotional pain diminishing, thank the crystal for its assistance. In the future, when you feel more capable of coping with the problem, retrieve it from the crystal. Hold the piece of smoky quartz to your heart again and let the old emotion flow back into you, lessened in impact and intensity by the passage of time.

✨ Use nine crystals to make nine wishes come true.

Perform this spell up to four times per year, preferably on the equinoxes and solstices. You'll need nine quartz crystals of similar sizes and shapes, plus a piece of heavy paper or cardboard. Draw a grid with nine squares on the paper and label them one through nine. On another piece of paper, write down nine wishes, one for each of the numbered squares. For example, wish number one might be for good health and wish two for prosperity. Set the paper on your altar, a table, or other flat surface with the squares facing up. Put one crystal on each square and ask it to help make the corresponding wish come true. After all nine crystals are in place, cover the whole thing with a piece of black or dark cloth and leave it overnight. In the morning, store your crystals and the paper grid until it's time to repeat the ritual. (NOTE: You may wish for the same nine things next time, if necessary, or make new requests.)

✼ Hang a prayer flag to send good luck to someone else.

The Tibetans imprint prayers on pieces of colorful cloth and hang these flags outside their temples, homes, and other places where the wind will cause them to flutter. As the flags blow in the wind, they release the prayers and carry them to the four corners of the Earth. You can follow this age-old tradition by making your own prayer flags to send blessings to someone you know or to people everywhere. According to magical belief, whatever you put out into the cosmic web comes back to you threefold, so the good wishes you send will bring good luck your way, too.

Cut out a piece of cloth and use a waterproof marker to write a prayer, wish, or blessing on it. The traditional colors for flags are red, green, yellow, and blue, but you may prefer to color-key your flag to the nature of your prayer, according to the guidelines on page 52. Hang the flag outside where the wind will catch it and carry your prayer to the person(s) you're praying for, whether it's yourself, another person, or beings in general. If you want to send an all-purpose blessing, the Serenity Prayer and Namasté blessing are good choices. I also have a prayer flag that says: "I am in harmony with Divine Will and all is well." Be creative, and hang as many flags as you like.

✿ Use a tarot card to make three wishes come true.

In the tarot, the nine of cups is sometimes referred to as the "wish card." When it appears in the "outcome" position in a reading, it shows that your hopes and dreams have a good chance of coming true. You can tap the energy of this lucky card by selecting it from a deck you don't ordinarily use, because you won't be returning it to the deck. On a piece of paper, write three wishes. Put this piece of paper behind the card, insert them into a picture frame, and hang it where you will see it often. Make sure to look at it for a few minutes every day, while you concentrate on your "wish list."

✪ Display the Wheel of Fortune tarot card.

Begin this spell on the first Thursday after the new moon and repeat it each day until the full moon. Select the Wheel of Fortune card from a tarot deck. This card symbolizes being in the right place at the right time to obtain good fortune. Display the card in a prominent place where you will see it often. Light sandalwood-, myrrh-, orange-, or cedar-scented incense. Stare at the tarot card for ten minutes while the incense burns and repeat an affirmation such as: "My life is rich with happiness, abundance, and good fortune of all kinds."

✥ Use the Sun tarot card to build confidence.

This spell can help you increase your self-confidence and sense of well-being. If possible, perform it outside in the sunshine. Remove the Sun card from a tarot deck and position it so that it sits upright facing you. Carve the astrological glyph for the sun into an orange or yellow candle, then place the candle beside the Sun card. Light the candle and, as it burns, focus your attention on the tarot card. Imagine the sun shining down on you (even if you are indoors), filling you with its radiance and life-giving energy. Sense your personal power increasing. After ten minutes, snuff out the candle. Repeat this spell as necessary, until your confidence is strengthened and you feel capable of handling the tasks before you.

✵ Sit in a circle of tarot cards to attract good fortune.

Remove the following cards from a tarot deck: the Sun (clarity, confidence), the Wheel of Fortune (good luck, opportunity), the Star (hope), the nine of cups (wishes fulfilled), the ten of pentacles (success), the three of cups (joy, celebration), and the World (rightness, harmony, balance). Lay these cards in a circle on the floor, then sit in the middle of the circle. Close your eyes and imagine the attributes symbolized by each card flowing toward you. Perform this ritual whenever you need a lift or for a few minutes each day to attract good fortune on a regular basis.

✪ Seek the aid of a totem animal.

In many shamanistic and magical traditions, spirit or totem animals are believed to possess certain powers. They can lend these to you when you need them. For instance, bears are known for their strength, foxes for cleverness, cheetahs for speed. To invoke the assistance of a totem animal, choose an animal that embodies the qualities you want to borrow. If you wish, find a picture of the animal in a book or magazine and focus on it for a few minutes.

Close your eyes, relax, and envision that animal standing before you. Ask it to share the traits you admire with you, then imagine the animal's characteristics flowing from it into you. You may also ask the animal to serve as your guide or guardian for a period of time. When you feel that you have blended the spirit animal's energy with your own, thank it and say good-bye. If you wish, you can keep an image of the totem animal nearby to remind you of its presence whenever you need it.

✿ Burn a light blue candle to encourage peace of mind.

Pale blue is associated with serenity—psychological studies show that sitting in a blue room can actually lower blood pressure, slow the pulse, and calm the nerves. With a nail or other sharp object, scratch *serenity* or *peace* into a blue candle. (Pillar candles are best for this purpose. If you like, select one scented with lavender or vanilla essential oil.) Light the candle and gaze into its flickering flame for ten minutes. Try to empty your mind of all thoughts and just relax. After ten minutes, snuff out the candle. Repeat this each day until the candle has burned down completely.

✡ **Burn an orange candle to stimulate good luck.**
This is a good spell to do if you have gotten in a rut and want to spark new, fortunate possibilities. Orange is associated with the element of fire, so it stimulates vitality, inspiration, and opportunity. Orange is also linked with Jupiter and the Sun, two of the most beneficent of the heavenly bodies. Use a nail or other tool to carve the words *good luck* in the side of an orange candle. Anoint the candle with essential oil of sweet orange, bergamot, cedar, or sandalwood, then light it and let it burn for ten minutes. As it burns, picture your heart and mind opening like doors to let blessings and opportunities enter your life. After ten minutes, snuff out the candle. Repeat this spell each day until your luck improves.

✬ Jump over a cauldron to improve your luck.

This magic ritual is often a part of the festivities on Beltane (May 1), but you can do it whenever you feel a need to improve your luck. The traditional method suggests that you build a fire in a magic cauldron and drop wishes into the flames as you leap over the burning cauldron, but this modified version is less risky and just as effective. Write a wish on a piece of paper, then light the paper on fire and drop it into your magic cauldron to finish burning. When the paper has burned completely, releasing your request into the cosmic web, and the flames have died down, carefully jump or step over the cauldron as you hold an image in your mind of your wish being fulfilled.

✿ Create a lucky sigil.

Configure the letters *L, U, C, K,* and *Y* into a design that you find appealing. The letters can be positioned upright, upside down, backwards, forwards—in any way you choose. Use uppercase or lowercase letters, or a combination of both. When you've finished creating your sigil, hang it in a place where you will see it often. Each time you look at it, you'll be reminded of your intention to attract good luck into your life. (For more about sigils, see Chapter 4.) If you prefer, you can add this sigil to a magical mojo or other good luck charm.

✡ String gemstones to attract the good things in life.

Long before they were prized for their material value, gemstones were worn as amulets and talismans. Each stone has its own properties and associations; by combining them correctly, you can improve your luck in every area. Use either a needle and thread or jeweler's wire to string nine different gemstone beads into a personal good luck charm: rose quartz for love, aventurine for prosperity, jade for health, and so on. Refer to Chapter 4 for a list of stones and their correspondences. Wear the beads as a necklace or bracelet. Or, if you'd rather, you can place all nine in a small leather pouch and carry it with you as a talisman.

✿ Burn a magical Yule fire to start off the year right.

Yule is celebrated at the winter solstice, which occurs around December 21. On this night, build a fire that contains nine varieties of wood. The Druids considered these trees sacred, so if possible, include some of them in your Yule fire: oak, ash, hazel, alder, birch, willow, holly, apple, yew, rowan, and hawthorn. When the fire has burned down completely, scoop up some of the ashes and wrap them in a piece of cloth. Place the packet under your pillow on the night of the solstice to bring good luck in the New Year.

✪ Draw a good-luck mandala — Spell 1.

A mandala is a circular image that symbolizes wholeness; it can be used in meditation, ritual, or magical spells to bring about desired conditions. Draw a circle and divide it into four quarters with a large **X**. This symbol is also the astrological glyph for the Part of Fortune, a lucky point in every birth chart. In each quadrant, sketch something that you wish to attract into your life. Don't worry about your artistic ability, just draw a symbol that represents this thing to you. For example, a heart might suggest love, a dollar sign could signify money, a peace symbol may stand for peace of mind. If you prefer, you can cut pictures from a magazine and paste them in the four sectors. When you're finished, say aloud three times: "I now attract these blessings into my life." Display the mandala where you will see it often.

✢ Draw a good-luck mandala — Spell 2.

Rather than asking for specific benefits, you create this mandala to establish harmony and happiness in your life by balancing the four elemental forces in the Universe. Draw a circle and divide it into four quarters with a large **X**, forming the astrological glyph for the Part of Fortune. In each quadrant, sketch something that represents one of the four elements: air, fire, water, and earth. If you prefer, you can cut pictures from magazines and paste them in the four sectors.

Make sure the images you choose show these elements in ways that convey joy, peace, or fruitfulness. For instance, you could select a picture of a blue, cloudless sky or rainbow for air; a welcoming hearth fire for fire; a lovely, calm lake for water; a field of flowers or apple trees laden with fruit for earth. As you fashion your magical mandala, imagine all the good things symbolized by these pictures flowing into your life from all directions. When you have finished, display your mandala in a place where you will see it often.

✿ Knot your wishes into a rope.

Light sage incense or bundled sage to clear the space in which you are working. Cut a piece of rope as long as you are tall. Think of up to nine blessings you want to attract into your life. Focus your attention fully on one of these and tie a knot into the rope. As you tie the knot, state this affirmation aloud: "This wish that I make now manifests in my life." Next, concentrate on the second wish as you tie another knot. Repeat the affirmation. Do this until you have tied a knot for each of your desires. Hold the rope in the incense smoke to charge it. Wear the rope around your waist for ten minutes each day until all of your requests have been fulfilled, then burn the rope.

✿ Take a magical bath to attract good luck.

Magicians often bathe before performing rituals or spells in order to calm and center themselves and to wash away unwanted vibrations. You can take a magical bath to put yourself in the right frame of mind to receive good luck, too. Run a tub of hot water and pour a few drops of bergamot, sweet orange, lavender, or vanilla essential oil into the water. Light an orange or yellow candle. As you soak in the hot water, visualize yourself opening up to all the good things the Universe has to offer. Imagine all obstacles and inner resistance washing away, leaving you ready to take advantage of fortunate opportunities. Spend at least ten minutes (or longer if you wish) envisioning happiness and good luck enriching your life in countless ways.

✩ Walk a labyrinth.

Many people walk labyrinths as a form of meditation or to gain insight and clarity. The center of the labyrinth is a power point that links you with heaven and earth. From this position, you can work powerful magic, communicate with other people, receive insights from other planes of existence, or send requests into the Universe. I perform most of my magic spells and rituals in my labyrinth to amplify their strength.

Walk into the center of a full-size labyrinth, if one is available for your use. If not, run your finger along the lines or "pathways" in the diagram below. Allow your mind to relax as you do this, and feel yourself becoming balanced and receptive. When you get to the center, focus all your attention on attracting happiness and good fortune into your life. If you have a specific request, ask it now. This is also a good time to chant an affirmation or say a prayer.

Walk back out of the labyrinth (or retrace the winding path in the diagram), knowing that the seed of your objective has been planted.

✿ Tap the energies of the earth and sky to enhance your happiness.

Being in sync with the Universe is the secret of happiness. This simple ritual lets you draw upon the energies of the earth and sky to achieve harmony and a sense of connectedness. If possible, perform this outside on a lovely, sunny day. Stand with your feet spread slightly so you feel balanced. Hold your arms outstretched at your sides with your right palm turned upward (toward the sky) and your left palm facing down (toward the earth). Close your eyes, take a few deep breaths, and relax. Imagine you are drawing down sky-energy with your right hand, and pulling up earth-energy with your left hand. Allow the vibrations to flow through your arms, into your body, so that they meet at your heart. Envision these energies circulating through your body, producing a sense of peace, joy, and well-being. Continue for a few minutes, or until your arms grow tired, then lower your arms and open your eyes. You'll feel both calm and revitalized.

✵ Make offerings to the deities in exchange for good luck.

Perform this ritual to show gratitude for the blessings and good fortune you have already received, and to encourage a continuous stream of luck to flow into your life. Choose a small object that you feel represents your intentions or that you believe will be appreciated by the deities that have helped you in the past. The offering need not be expensive; the thought is what counts. Offer this token by tossing it into a body of water, hanging it from a tree, or burying it in the ground. As you do this, say or think a few words of thanks and ask your favorite deity to continue bringing you good fortune in the future.

✡ **Write a story with a happy ending.**

Writers use their imaginations to create life according to their own designs, and you can, too. Because the essence of magic involves forming a mental picture of something and imbuing it with emotion, creative writing is the perfect magical format. How do you want your life to turn out? Write a short story in which you are the protagonist. Describe all the wonderful things that happen to you, in as much detail as possible. Really try to "get into" the character—it's you, after all. Don't worry about grammar, syntax, spelling, or other details. You aren't going to read this story to anyone else or submit it for publication. The important thing is to show good fortune coming to you and to feel joy in the process of creating your story—and your life.

Resources

Alexander, Skye. *Magickal Astrology*. Franklin Lakes, NJ: Career Press/New Page Books, 2000.

Alexander, Skye. *10-Minute Crystal Ball*. Gloucester, MA: Fair Winds Press/Rockport Publishers, 2002.

Beyerl, Paul. *The Master Book of Herbalism*. Custer, WA: Phoenix Publishing, 1984.

Bills, Rex E. *The Rulership Book: A Directory of Astrological Correspondences*. Richmond, VA: Macoy Publishing and Masonic Supply, 1971.

Fortune, Dion. *Sane Occultism*. London: Rider & Co., 1929.

Green, Marian. *The Elements of Ritual Magic*. Dorset, England: Element Books, 1990.

Kraig, Donald Michael. *Modern Magick: Eleven Lessons in the High Magickal Arts*. St. Paul, MN: Llewellyn Publications, 1999.

Mella, Dorothee L. *Stone Power*. New York, NY: Warner Books, 1986.

Starhawk. *The Spiral Dance: A Rebirth of the Ancient Religion of the Great Goddess*. New York, NY: Harper & Row, 1979.

Tisserand, Robert B. *The Art of Aromatherapy*. Rochester, VT: Healing Arts Press, 1977.

Watson, Nancy B. *Practical Solitary Magic*. York Beach, ME: Samuel Weiser, 1996.

About the Author

Skye Alexander is the author of *10-Minute Feng Shui* and *10-Minute Crystal Ball*; two astrology books, *Magickal Astrology* and *Planets in Signs*; and the mystery novel *Hidden Agenda*, which won the 1998 Kiss of Death Award for the year's best book of romantic suspense. A contributing author to *Your Birthday Sign through Time* and *A Taste of Murder*, she has also written for numerous magazines and newspapers, as well as for TV and radio. Her short stories have appeared in literary magazines and anthologies. She appeared in a Discovery Channel special on magic, performing a ritual at Stonehenge. She lives in Massachusetts with her cat, Domino.